The Most Common Entrepreneurial Mistakes and How to Avoid Them

The Most Common Entrepreneurial Mistakes and How to Avoid Them

Lisa J. MacDonald

BEP

BUSINESS EXPERT PRESS

Leader in applied, concise business books

The Most Common Entrepreneurial Mistakes and How to Avoid Them

First published in 2023 by
Business Expert Press, LLC
222 East 46th Street, New York, NY 10017
www.businessexpertpress.com

ISBN-13: 978-1-63742-473-5 (paperback)
ISBN-13: 978-1-63742-474-2 (e-book)

Business Expert Press Entrepreneurship and Small Business Management Collection

First edition: 2023

10 9 8 7 6 5 4 3 2 1

Description

Masterclass in Entrepreneurial Development

We all want to be in charge of our own lives, but what happens when the game of business keeps changing?

How can you successfully find new clients, beat the competition, and do it on a shoestring budget?

Lisa J. MacDonald has coached 1000s of business owners for over 25 years, has a PhD in the school of hard knocks, and is the mother of 8. In *The Most Common Entrepreneurial Mistakes and How to Avoid Them*, she uncovers proven cutting-edge business principles to quickly shift entrepreneurs from overwhelm and confusion to confidently fulling their vision sustainably.

You will learn the following:

- Charge what you're worth and get the revenue you deserve.
- Attract the right clients over and over again.
- Unleash business possibilities hidden in your network.
- Uncover the key trends in your industry to keep you ahead of the competition.
- Bounce back strong and robust no matter the changes in the market.

Your successful business is waiting for you. You don't have to go at it alone. Get this state-of-the-art research-based step-by-step guide that will show you exactly how to get unstuck, attract your best clients, and fulfill your vision.

Keywords

best business practices; common business mistakes for entrepreneurs; entrepreneur business growth; small business growth; best business tips; advanced entrepreneur advice; strategic business plan; how to grow a business; how to build a company; how to be an entrepreneur; entrepreneur life; business development entrepreneur

Contents

Testimonials ix

Acknowledgments xi

Introduction xiii

Section 1   **The Most Common Mistakes, Detours, and Unexpected Surprises That Over 50 Entrepreneurs Made in Growing Their Business** 1

Chapter 1   Rocky Mindset: Potholes, Dips, and Fractures Resulting From Faulty Perception 3

Chapter 2   Neglecting to Do One's Homework: Unprepared, Not Competitive, and Failing to Know What Will Be on the Exam 35

Chapter 3   Lacking Marketing/Sales Know How 57

Chapter 4   Stepping Into the Quicksand of Poor Relationship Skills 81

Section 2   **Four Core Principles Every Business Expert Wishes They Knew From the Start** 105

Chapter 5   Transform Into a Business Growing Machine 107

Chapter 6   Building Powerful Relationships 123

Section 3   **Pulling It All Together** 141

Chapter 7   Baby-Stepping Around Mistakes and Toward Success 143

Conclusion 149

Appendix: Checklist of Action Steps 151

About the Author 157

Index 159

Testimonials

"Lisa's book is rooted in the lived experiences of 50 business owners, which gives life and vitality to all the many on-point business lessons. But Lisa doesn't just stop at lessons; the exercises she's included at the end of each chapter are a masterclass in entrepreneurial development. Do them and watch yourself (and your business) grow!"—**Linda Claire Puig, AdventurousLife.io, 6FigureNewsletters.com**

"Lisa J. MacDonald managed to culminate the experiences of entrepreneurs and business owners into a book encompassing the lessons earned and the wisdom of attending years of masterclasses, courses, and reading other books. This is a must-read for new and seasoned people in business."—**Marcey Rader, Founder, RaderCo**

*"*The Most Common Entrepreneurial Mistakes and How to Avoid Them *is an essential read for anyone interested in starting or growing a business. MacDonald's years of experience in the business world make her uniquely qualified to identify the most common mistakes entrepreneurs make and offer advice on how to avoid them. If you're looking for a roadmap to success, this book is a great place to start."*—**Lisa Jones RDN, Speaker, Author, and Humorist at LisaJonesLIVE**

"Wow. I was blown away. This is a very insightful guide for just about any entrepreneur. In fact, I wish I had read this before I started my arduous business journey. MacDonald did a wonderful job of combining real-world experiences with empirical research."—**Dr. Lynne Hill, Psy.D**

"Forget those boring business books filled with a ton of theory aimed at corporate. The Most Common Entrepreneur Mistakes *is the needed book for entrepreneurs. It is written with a deeply practical and intuitive understanding of their problems and how to overcome them. MacDonald is a seasoned veteran. Read it. You'll be glad you did!"*—**Ann Naimark, MFT, author of** *A Touch of Light*

"I loved this book because it wasn't only about the coaches' experience and knowledge. It included the wisdom of successful entrepreneurs from many different industries, which helped broaden the scope. This awesome business guide outlines solid principles that will work in any business. It definitely made me wish I had this when I first started my busines15 years ago!"
—Stephanie Beeby, CEO of In Flow Consulting

Acknowledgments

To Nigel Watts who sought me out and encouraged me to put together a business proposal and still believed in this project when the publishing world was hit hard from the effects of COVID. This book wouldn't be without you. To Scott Isenberg who also saw the possibility and to Richard MacDonald for being my rock and BG Peck for his amazing insight and passion for business.

Unless there is a direct name given, gender and professions and other identifiable characteristics and traits have been changed to protect privacy.

Introduction

The international business climate is experiencing dramatic changes in which more people worldwide are exploring the options of small business and entrepreneurship in unprecedented numbers. But, as statistical data shows, many of these want-to-be owners fail.[1]

The reasons vary from lack of funding, lack of understanding their market, not niching their services properly, to not having a sustainable sales funnel. Most people launch their new pursuit with confidence in their trade skills but lack many of the foundational tools for operating their endeavor. As a business coach, I wanted to find an accurate view of what is working in the current environment. I interviewed over 50 successful business owners who weathered the 2008 crisis well in 50 different industries to see what worked for them and what didn't during an economic downturn. I also interviewed over 20 more entrepreneurs in 2022 to find out what fundamentals have changed (none of them did). You will find quotes from some of those entrepreneurs throughout the book highlighting their biggest mistakes and how they turned them around to ultimately be successful.

The research revealed the most common universal mistakes made and how to avoid them. From there, it became clear the core fundamental principles that are a must to implement for the best chance to succeed. This book points out what those entrepreneurs did to survive recessions, other upsets, and how to ride an ever-changing market. The principles are based on the real-life experience of those who are succeeding in their business and chosen industry.

The chapters provide practical, simple actions that are easy to follow and can have a big impact on the results. You will find in each section an Application Corner with steps on how you can immediately customize and apply best practices to help you keep on track.

---

[1] A. Enfory. February 5, 2022. "The Ultimate List of Small Business Statistics for 2022." www.adamenfroy.com/small-business-statistics.

People, when it boils down to it, are people and often make the same mistakes unless they make a deliberate effort to avoid them. That is why I am so excited to share this important and relevant information with you—my hope and wish is you will not just read this information and think, "Oh, that is nice." My hope is you will absorb the insights and look for ways you are guilty or ways to avoid these pitfalls if you are just starting out. Most of the time, it is hard to see if you are making the mistake by approaching your work with theory. The entrepreneur needs to be in the game to really uncover the sticky points and to receive immediate feedback from the market.

If you listen to the mistakes that others have made and then apply what is relevant, you can completely transform your business, yourself, and your life.

The mistakes highlighted might not appear exactly like what you are doing. You will need creativity and open-mindedness to see how a concept relates to your unique situation. To receive the most out of this book and to harvest more of the results you are striving for, be courageous enough to examine your business and operations from various angles and lenses. If you haven't started yet, use that courage to analyze your idea and strategy that you are thinking about.

I have seen people take this information, digest it, apply it to their own circumstances, make adjustments, and double or triple their income in a few months, working 30 percent less. More importantly, after applying these powerful principles, they have moved from suffering, feeling bad about themselves to feeling more confident and more at ease with their work. The by-product was a solid foundation that established a powerful structure and strategy that allowed them to show up in the marketplace successfully.

If you come to the book completely committed to looking honestly at yourself and your company, you can't help but grow. So, let's dive into what mistakes other successful entrepreneurs and small business owners made along their way and how you can avoid them.

The Most Common Mistakes, Detours, and Unexpected Surprises That Over 50 Entrepreneurs Made in Growing Their Business

CHAPTER 1

Rocky Mindset: Potholes, Dips, and Fractures Resulting From Faulty Perception

One thing I know from working with thousands of entrepreneurs in the past 25 years is that each person is unique, has special gifts, and operates just a little differently. Despite that uniqueness and the dynamics of diverse industries, variables, and culture, almost every entrepreneur suffers from periodic doubt. It would be almost impossible not to. The only sure thing in entrepreneurship is RISK.

When an entrepreneur seizes onto an idea, a dream, and pursues it to make it a reality, there is no guarantee that they will make it. It is scary taking the leap risking finances, reputation, and time for an idea.

Most entrepreneurs who have been in the game for a while trust that self-employment is less risky than being at the mercy of corporate layoff, unseen change of management, and the illusion of a steady paycheck. Some of them expressed that they would rather fail at attempting something great or worthwhile than be in a "job."

What the successful entrepreneur knows is the results they produce running their business starts and ends with them and that means there is always something that they can do about the outcomes they are producing. To have the ability to shift, making changes when needed, is less risky than to put their fate in the hands of another institution or company.

So how does an entrepreneur steady their mindset, stay confident, and give themselves the best chance for success? Time to find out.

Mistake #1: Didn't Believe in Self, Others, and Your Company

When asked what she wished she had known before starting her company, one business owner reported that she would have loved to know if she'd be profitable. If she had known that, she wouldn't have wasted all that time stressing. The knowledge that she had achieved success would have saved her a lot of worry, energy, and health concerns.

It is easy to say, "Don't stress. Don't worry." But when you are building your business, your dream, and sometimes when you have your whole family's survival dependent on your success, it is not so easy. Add to that the doubt that often occurs when taking huge steps you've never taken before. You don't automatically know if you have the ability to soar. It's a mystery. This is part of the fun, part of the terror, and part of the risk.

Of course, it is natural to doubt, but if there is more than just a small bit, and if you entertain the worry, you are draining energy that you could put into your business. This scattered energy will not be serving you. For this small business owner, she figured out worrying about whether she was good enough was a waste of her focus and hurt her efforts. She wasn't going to suddenly have a "good enough" stamp slapped on her forehead.

She saw how entertaining those worries were hurting her. At the time, she was hosting an event. So instead of stressing about wondering if the launch campaign would work, she resolved to hop on the phone and call prospects until she filled the event. She was going to keep taking action until she was successful. And that was what she did. She called and called and called until she reached the numbers she needed for the event. She shifted from failure to success by refusing to entertain the doubt and switching into action. Being in constant action doesn't guarantee everything will work, but staying in doubt guarantees your business growth will experience a major drag.

This idea taps into the basic idea of stoicism. The entrepreneur "does everything he can to hit the target, but his happiness does not depend on whether he hits the target or not (Stobaeus 2, 76, 11–15)."[1] What matters is the action the doer takes.

---

[1] J. Sellars. July 23 2016. "Stoicism and the Art of Archery by John Sellars," *Modern Stoicism.* https://modernstoicism.com/stoicism-and-the-art-of-archery/.

If you aren't getting the results in your business you want, and you are pointing the finger at someone else for the reason why, you are blaming. If you are pointing the finger at yourself, then you are shaming.

What is a healthier approach? Objectively examine your business and figure out where the breakdown is. Perhaps you are saying, "It's so-and-so's fault that we aren't growing faster. They don't get that..." or perhaps you are saying, "I can't figure out the technology...."

When you find yourself doing this, stop. Instead, search for where the bottleneck is. What needs to happen to achieve better results.

If you are lacking money, then it is a sales problem. Determine where in your sales process you are hitting the snag. Not enough sales calls? That is a prospecting issue. Not enough people saying yes, then look at your sales skills. Don't have time to bring on another client? You have a structure issue, and it's time to explore ways to scale.

If instead you are struggling with technology, then you need to either increase your skills or bring on tech support or both.

Another area that frequently comes up with beliefs getting in the way is the owner knows what the big next step in their business is, but they hold themselves back because they believe that they can't do it. They tell themselves stories to rationalize and prove why they should not do what is scaring them. For example, one I hear a lot, and one I have told myself, is that I can't do marketing. Or another common one is I can't do technology. There is just no way I can figure that out.

To break this pattern:

1. Catch yourself feeling scared or resistant to do something.
2. Notice if you come up with reasons why you shouldn't or can't do it.
3. Write down the reasons you believe you can't.
4. See if you can think of two or three examples of ways that statement you just wrote down is *not* true. Almost always you end up realizing that taking the next step is not as big of a deal as you thought.
5. When you uncover the negative beliefs, look for what the truth is really.

   For example, when I voiced that I was lousy at marketing, my mentor asked me questions about my market and the results I was producing. The facts were I was writing copy and making sales. Could I improve? Of course, was I lousy...the results were saying I wasn't.

My belief needed updating. A lot of us need to update our beliefs. Often, we were bad at something at one point, but somewhere along the journey, we improved and didn't realize it. Conscious awareness is needed to notice these changes that often evolve so gradually we don't catch that we are improving.

What do you do if the truth is you really aren't good at something? Great question. Google the answer. Find help. Take a class or hire someone. We are so interconnected we can find the answer.

In fact, Harvard did a case study on the effects of fear on the entrepreneur and how to capitalize on that fear.

Not Capitalizing on the Useful Nature of Fear

Fear is a constant element of being an entrepreneur. According to the research done by James Hayon and Gariella Cacciotti, fear is often prevalent with the sixty-five founders that they interviewed. The trick wasn't whether the founder was afraid or not, but how they dealt with it.

In the case study, Hayon and Cacciotti found the type of fear the entrepreneur focused on determined their outcome. Some types of fear would motivate the entrepreneur toward taking actions that would move them toward success. Other types of fear acted like a hinderance and stopped action. The study mentions that being aware of the fear and how it affected the entrepreneur was critical in how it impacted their results.[2] For additional information on this read about Jim Collin's ideas about "productive paranoia" in his book *Great by Choice*.[3]

Motivating fear came when the entrepreneur focused on areas they could do something about—money issues, pursuit of opportunities, and other elements that persistence would determine the outcome.

When the fear slowed down the entrepreneur, the attention was more on the person's abilities or value. Hayton and Cacciotti's research echoed my own that many seasoned entrepreneurs wished that when they first

---

[2] J. Hayton and G. Cacciotti. April 3, 2018. "How Fear Helps (and Hurts) Entrepreneurs," [online] *Harvard Business Review*. https://hbr.org/2018/04/how-fear-helps-and-hurts-entrepreneurs.

[3] J. Collins. 2011. *Great by Choice* (Random House).

started out, they didn't worry so much if they were going to make it. They wish they had spent more of their energy on doing what it takes. This concept echoes Carol Dweck's landmark work showing success is determined by a person's mindset. If a person has a fixed mindset—believes that their skills, abilities, and talent are set in stone—they are less likely to move forward. If a person has a growth mindset—believes that their skills, abilities, talents can change through effort—they are more likely to be successful.[4]

The findings of the various researches on how entrepreneurs deal with failure suggests if the entrepreneur interprets the failure as a personal fault, they don't bounce back as quickly. In Susan Peppercorn's article "How to Overcome Your Fear of Failure," she points out that the individual often takes responsibility for the all the outcome when it is outside their control. Being overly responsible for outcomes inhibits the entrepreneur. When the focus is on something that no one has control over, it increases stress and can lead to a hostile work environment.[5]

Stopping the Overresponsible Trigger

One way to counter the overly responsible tendency that many entrepreneurs slip into is by carefully judging your performance. I often coach clients not to look at their business efforts based on things they do not have control over. For example, whether a person buys their product, if they are hired, and so forth. Instead to determine whether they are being successful by looking at whether they took action or not.

If they showed up and gave a speech, they won. If they made the sales call, they won. If they sent out that nurture e-mail to their newsletter list, they won.

If they took action, they won. Could they do it better next time? Of course. And that will happen naturally as the entrepreneur gains experience and receives feedback from the results their actions produce.

---

[4] C.S. Dweck. 2006. *Mindset* (Random House).
[5] S. Peppercorn. December 10, 2018. "How to Overcome Your Fear of Failure," *Harvard Business Review*. https://hbr.org/2018/12/how-to-overcome-your-fear-of-failure.

Being in the game and trying is winning. A common motto is "time in the market matters much more than trying to time the market." You won't know what is possible without taking action and learning from what happens. Growth is the result of action. If you are stuck striving to make it perfect and blaming yourself for things you have no control over, you are either slowed or stopped.

According to Josh Linkner's research, more success and momentum were produced both for corporations and entrepreneurs by creating small experiments of actions, receiving feedback, and trying again than spending lots of time working to make everything perfect the first round.[6]

Overall, fear is a part of being an entrepreneur. Entrepreneurs take risks, with no guarantees. If you see fear as part of the learning process and continue to stay in action, adjusting with the knowledge you gleaned, fear will serve as a positive motivator.

Doubt and Other Ways You Are Stopping Yourself

Many times, when entrepreneurs doubt themselves, they are listening to a voice in their head saying unhelpful messages like their family resents them for being so busy. Or they are not smart enough or good enough to figure something out. Or they are taking too much of a risk and will lose all this money and be worse off for trying.

The ruminations drain their productivity and leave them with less energy to focus on their business. Research also suggests that this doubt lowers self-esteem.[7] Sometimes people experience self-doubt as a way to avoid confronting new goals. That inner voice says things like: "I don't know if I can do this." "Oh, this is really scary." "Maybe I shouldn't do this."

Or the scariest one of all, "Maybe I should get a real job." So why do we do this? The saboteur (the negative voice in our head) wants us to stay the same. He (the saboteur) is unwilling to go outside of his comfort

---

[6] J. Linkner. 2021. *Big Little Breakthroughs* (Simon and Schuster).

[7] Q. Zhao, A. Wichman, and E. Frishberg. March 24, 2019. "Self-Doubt Effects Depend on Beliefs About Ability: Experimental Evidence." https://pubmed.ncbi.nlm.nih.gov/30907262/.

zone. In fact, he's scared of change. If he compels us to stop moving forward or to go slower, the saboteur wins and our confidence lessens. If we replace the negative voices with positive ones, eventually the negative voices settle.

Shirzad Chamine, best-selling author of *Positive Intelligence* and lecturer at Stanford, interviewed 100 chief executive officers (CEOs)-about how they viewed themselves after a long day at work. What he found was that the CEOs suffered from the negative voices too. He claims that everyone has positive and negative voices running through their minds. Through his work, he found the best way to perform is when the mind "is calm, centered, focused, able to see possibilities."[8]

Being able to calm our minds, being focused, and see the potential is not an easy task.

We have the tendency to have negative thinking habits.[9] Many times, what is needed is updating your mental files of how you see yourself or take on the belief that it was the way it was "until now" then do what you need to do to change the situation.

Sometimes, our environment has a powerful effect on the way we see ourselves. A negative environment is dangerous because it can zap your success energy. We will be going into the influence environment has on you later in the book.

How to shift out of a negative loop? Recognize the truth of your situation. Dale Carnegie encourages the worrier to ask what is the absolute worst thing that can happen. Accept that as a possibility then work to stop it. The theory behind this is that worry dissipates when we face head on what could happen and then strive to build a better outcome. One way to make the outcome better is to surround yourself with people that support you, such as a great business coach, mastermind group, or accountability partner. Securing possibility thinkers for your team is also very helpful.

---

[8] L. Stangel. August 2017 "Shirzad Chamine: Five Strategies to Challenge Negative Thoughts." www.gsb.stanford.edu/insights/shirzad-chamine-five-strategies-challenge-negative-thoughts.

[9] B. Verplanken, O. Friborg, and C.E. Wang. March 2007. "Mental Habits: Metacognitive Reflection on Negative Self-Thinking." https://pubmed.ncbi.nlm.nih.gov/17352607/.

The Positive Side of Doubt

Research[10] has also found that doubting has distinct advantages. In the study "A Neuropsychological Test of Belief and Doubt," the researchers found that doubt helps people make better money and purchase decisions. Doubt causes us to access risk and look for possible downside of moving forward. Doubt prompts us to use critical thinking when determining our decisions and to not just float on wishful thinking.

Power Strategy of Support to Shore Up the Rocky Mindset

In Hayton and Cacciotti's research, they found what you focus on as a founder is critical to whether fear is positioned to work for you or against you. This is an important element of your business to pay consistent attention to. It is easy to become caught up in the day-to-day operations and not notice how you are making decisions. At the heart of entrepreneurship, the founder is the responsible one. If the business is going well, that's on you. If the business is experiencing hiccups, that's on you. If the market changes, it's on you to adapt—or your business goes under. Gulp.

It is a lot to manage. Win or lose what happens in your business and the results achieved rest on your shoulders. In the Hayton and Cacciotti study, they mention the importance of having the support of networks and mentors. This taps into the critical element of surrounding yourself with the right kind of backing.

Personally, I have tracked my business growth to see what I was able to achieve on my own versus when I surrounded myself with supportive like-minded people. Without me even realizing it, my income tripled when I was in a supportive container.

Part of the reason this happened was the mentor in the group demanded I triple the prices I charged. The group echoed the value that I offered and pointed out how I was selling myself short. Wanting to be

---

[10] E. Asp, K. Manzel, B. Koestner, C.A. Cole, N.L. Denburg, and D. Tranel. July 9, 2012. "A Neuropsychological Test of Belief and Doubt: Damage to Ventromedial Prefrontal Cortex Increases Credulity for Misleading Advertising." www.ncbi.nlm.nih.gov/pmc/articles/PMC3391647/.

the good student, I immediately asked for more on the sales calls, and to my shock, the prospects signed up with me. In two months, I was able to earn more than I had in whole year.

Another benefit I received in the group was one sunny summer day my mentor took me aside. We were at a mastermind retreat and had only talked on the phone before then. He said to me, "Lisa, there is something about you and who you are that doesn't come across on the phone or in your writing. You have an energy about you that people only experience when being in your presence." He fell quiet. "You need to do video. That is the only way people will experience your energy."

Well, that one bit of advice simplified my marketing path greatly.

A seasoned mentor has the ability to drill down to the core issue or the customized path for the entrepreneur. I have seen this kind of guidance and support transforms many businesses.

Application Corner

Exercise #1: Business Spot Check

To receive the most out of this book, apply these principles to yourself and your business. You probably don't have the same struggles I have mentioned, but you likely have areas preventing you from reaching the next level. Grab a pen and paper and figure out where fear is slowing you down.

Answer the following questions:

What do you worry about when it comes to your business?
How much time do you spend worrying?
What would have to change for you to no longer worry?
What would you need to do to lessen the worry and shift into productive action?

Go through your list and determine which fear you can do something about and which one is more of a personal evaluation.

If the concern is something you can do something about, label that concern as "A" (Action).

If the concern is more centered on your personal value or the value of your idea, label those concerns as "P" (Personal).

For all A worries, come up with a battle plan on how you will meet the current challenge.
Example:

Worry: I am worried I won't make enough sales to meet my bills.
Battleplan: Attend a networking meeting and set up at least five sales calls a week.

For all the P worries, come up with a battle plan on how you are going to change your focus or your belief system to support your efforts. Asking this question might help you shift your focus:
How can I change my focus to something I can do something about?

Example: I must be a failure. I am not bringing in enough money.
Questions to Inspire a Shift: What do I need to learn or do to make my company more profitable?
New Belief: I don't have time to worry about whether I am a failure. I need to hop on the phone and make sales calls until I cover the financial bleed.
New Belief with a Battleplan: I am going to learn more about how to identify my perfect client and be more attractive to them so they seek me out for work. I got this. I am just learning this skill now, but I'll figure it out. I always do.

Exercise #2: Pop Quiz on Your Ability to Feel Confident

When you picture yourself standing in front of your raving fans and they are all applauding your efforts, what do you feel?
Do you want to shrink and hide?
Do you feel boastful?
Or do you feel a deep gratitude for being able to serve the people you have?

Work on this visualization until you have the reaction that would most benefit your growth and the people you serve.

Exercise #3: Shifting Negative Beliefs

If you are struggling with a negative view of yourself in business, or in other areas of your life, try this exercise.

What negative thoughts do you have about yourself?
Examples:

I can't do marketing.
I am too shy to do sales.
I don't do videos well.

Where did this belief come from?
Example:

I can't do marketing because …
    the first time I did a promotion no one bought.
I am too shy to do sales because …
    every time I try to sell, I don't know what to say, and my face gets red, and my heart feels like it will pound out of my chest.
I don't do video well because …
    the first time I was on a Zoom call during the pandemic my clothes were all wrong. My hair looked lifeless. The lighting washed out my face, and I had no idea where to look.

What evidence suggests this negative view is faulty?
I can't do marketing.
    Well, I do have clients, so I must have done marketing well enough at some point.
I am too shy to do sales.
    Sometimes I do talk about what I do, but it's more of a conversation not a sales call. I can handle talking to one person about something I am passionate about.

I don't do video well.

I did make it on that Zoom call, so I guess I do do video. I just have things to learn.

What can you do today to change your perception?

I can't do marketing.

I am going to repeat that promotion that worked and see if it will work again.

I am too shy to do sales.

At the next networking meeting, I am going to talk to George. I know he needs my service. I will just ask him what he is doing to fix that problem and tell him how my services can help.

I don't do video well.

I will ask my granddaughter to help me set up my video. She loves this stuff. She would have fun going through my wardrobe to find the best camera-ready outfits. This could be fun.

Resources

Collins, J.C. 2011. *Great by Choice*. Random House.

Dweck, C.S. 2016. *Mindset: The New Psychology of Success*. Random House.

Linkner, J. 2021. *Big Little Breakthroughs: How Small, Everyday Innovations Drive Oversized Results*. Post Hill Press.

Sutherland, J. and J.V. Sutherland. 2014. *Scrum*. Currency.

Mistake #2: Didn't Know Your Value

Not knowing your value is a big mistake that many of the business owners I interviewed brought up. These owners reported that it would have been highly beneficial and would have saved them a lot of suffering if they had known at the beginning of launching their business the value they brought to the marketplace.

This is tricky. To understand the contribution, what we offer is something that has to be worked on throughout our career. We wear blinders to ourselves and the impact we have on others. An excellent way to uncover what you bring to the table is asking your clients what value they receive from your services or products. Or listen to them when they describe your impact on them, whether they share this verbally or through client testimonials.

Most of the time the entrepreneur is shocked at what their clients say. When I did this exercise, my clients told me the main reason they worked with me wasn't my knowledge base but the fact I had gone through a lot of hard events in my life, such as domestic violence, health issues, deaths, and learning disabilities. They felt I would understand their challenges. They liked the tangible results I was able to help them achieve, too, but they reported that as a plus not the main reason they worked with me. They claimed who I was and what I had been through took their excuses away from them and made them step it up in their own lives and business. That was nowhere near what I thought I offered, but I listened, then changed my brand and my marketing to reflect what they valued.

One of the men I interviewed found to his great surprise that the main reason he had women clients was because they felt safe around him and sensed that they could trust him. Another male thought his value was his high-tech skill, which was part of his value, but another part he didn't know was his ability to talk "guy talk" and help the men forget about their troubles. A female interviewed thought it was her experience with an illness in the family and her ability to cope with it, when in fact it was that she was a unifier and connected to vast communities.

None of these reasons was what the business owner thought it was. When the male business owner learned that his secret weapon was the fact women felt safe around him, he was able to step more into who he was naturally and attract more female clients. The male who could guy code showed up to events and did a YouTube show using his natural gift for guy code, packing his calendar with clients. The female business owner capitalized on her community connections and was able to forge relationships with prominent influencers.

Some entrepreneurs mentioned that it took them a long time to realize the tool or the outcome they were offering wasn't the biggest value, but it was the emotional benefits from working with that entrepreneur. Many of us stay loyal to service providers who treat us well. Current research shows that customers and clients who feel valued and respected while doing business with you is the critical factor for customer loyalty.[11]

Another reason we are often blind to our own contribution, influence, and impact is because we operate in our expertise and have been doing so for a long time. Our knowledge and skills feel commonplace to us. We often forget what it was like not knowing or having the skills we now have. We have become unconsciously competent.

In the first stage, you aren't even aware that you don't have the knowledge or skill or why that skill is important. The second stage is where you are aware you don't have the skills and are aware of the need for them. Third stage is you are actively learning the skill, and the fourth stage, you are moving toward mastery.[12]

The trouble happens for the entrepreneur when they assume everyone knows what they are offering. A simple example of this was when I first started teaching at a community college, I believed that since most of my students were born with the iPhone existing, they were good with computers.

Granted, a lot of my students were, but there were many who struggled navigating with an online portal. When I figured out my assumption was wrong, I took the class through instructions on how to use the online platform. The struggling students reported value in that instruction, just

---

[11] N. Millard, T. Coe, M. Gardner, A. Gower, L. Hole, and S. Crowle. 2000. "The Future of Customer Contact," *BT Technology Journal* 18, pp. 51–52. https://doi.org/10.1023/A:1026549115555.

[12] "The Four Stages of Competence." n.d. www.mccc.edu/~lyncha/documents/stagesofcompetence.pdf (accessed April 9, 2022).

as I found the student in the class who fixed my tech challenges with the white-board valuable.

Value is determined by the receiver not the giver.

Additionally, entrepreneurs who don't know their value might assume what they have to offer isn't what others need. As a result, they will try to bring something else to the marketplace that they are not an expert in. Promoting information or delivering something you are not an expert in is never a good idea.

Another symptom of not understanding your value is putting too much information in your webinars, online courses, presentations, newsletters, and advertisements. This onslaught overwhelms the prospect, client, or listener. The entrepreneur does this out of a belief that they need to pack value into the presentation when often less is more.

It is critical to understand the unique value you give the marketplace. To find this out, write down your thoughts, ask others, and research your industry. See if what you think makes you different is seconded by your customers. Dig.

Entrepreneurs who don't know their value don't know their customer's problems. When you can see your customers' problems clearly, and what you can do to provide assistance to the problem, then your confidence in your own value increases.

By you knowing the core level how your product or service helps and is valued by others, everything is easier. Easier for you as a business owner and easier for your clients to know what to expect from engaging with your company. Knowing your contribution dramatically reduces the tension of asking for the sale. When you have something that you know is regarded by the client more highly than the price you charge, and you've seen other clients experience the significance repeatedly, sales feel more like giving a service than prospecting. This knowledge of your value makes marketing smoother because you know what your potential customers want.

This is one of those principles of business that you can't skip over if you want to be successful. Everyone is different and has different things to offer. To find your value and uniqueness takes focus but is well worth the effort.

Owning Your Value Directly Affects Your Prices

Another place your sense of value is reflected is in the prices you charge for your services or product. Yes, market-driven pricing is a factor but the psychological part of pricing also impacts the entrepreneur's ability to charge.

One entrepreneur stated that his problem owning his value had been around pricing. He declared, "When the confidence comes, your prices increase." At the root of most undercharging is the lack of belief in the value provided. The confidence doesn't come until the entrepreneur understands what it is they actually do.

Asking for what you are worth can be a challenge for some entrepreneurs. They don't want to take advantage of others. The way to deal with that objection is to not take advantage of the customer but to see and understand the value you are giving the customer and to give even more value.

When the entrepreneur fully understands the value they give to the customer or client, it becomes easier for them to stand in what they offer. If they don't stand in their value and continue to undercharge most entrepreneurs will not stay in business for very long.

Tim Stobierski, contributing writer for Harvard Online Business School, explores the various components of value-based marketing.[13] With his approach to marketing, the business looks at the customers' willingness to pay, the cost of production, and the margin for the business.

If an entrepreneur is just starting out and has no idea what to charge, doing market research on a fair price is a good beginning point. It is helpful to know the wide range of prices and what is being offered. When there is no clear price range, charge what you think the service or product is worth and beta test the response. Does the product or service sell easily? Time to up the price. If sales are low (or nonexistent), then you might have a price problem.

Often a good way to build confidence is to begin with a lower price. Test market your service. After the initial experiment, if you are able to collect testimonials proving that people find merit, increase the price.

---

[13] T. Stobierski. November 3, 2020. "A Beginner's Guide to Value-Based Strategy." https://online.hbs.edu/blog/post/value-based-strategy.

For many entrepreneurs, owning their value comes with getting in the game and trying it out. Seeing the results, their confidence and understanding grow.

Application Corner

Exercise #1: Uncover Your Uniqueness

Write down the value your company offers. Drill down to as specific detail as possible.

Now determine what you offer to your clients or customers. Keep going until you know what you bring is unique and valuable and is marketable. You may need to consider many different variables, from location to package services to personal talents to unique products to appealing cost values—you get the idea.

Exercise #2: Interviewing Prospects for Their Problems

Interview at least 10 to 15 prospects that you think would be ideal clients. In the interview, you are trying to uncover their core problems and the language they use to describe them. In product design circles, they call this type of research as "problem space."

The better you know the struggles of the clients, the easier it is to show them that you are valuable because of your solutions.

Exercise #3: Interviews for Value

One of the best ways to uncover your value is to call your clients and ask them what they think. Talk to at least 10 clients or past clients:

What value are they receiving from your work together?
Why did they decide to work with you instead of someone else?
What made you stand apart?
How has the client's life/production/work changed through your time
     together?

Make sure you document their answers for later review.

Once the interviews are done, review your notes and recordings. Look for the common patterns. What did your clients say over and over again? When you see the pattern and hear from them and the value they received, make sure that is reflected in your marketing and sales efforts. Nothing sells people like hearing marketing that speaks to the heart of their problem in their language.

Exercise #4: Uncover Value in Client Sessions

If you are a service provider who has sessions or classes with your clients, another good way to find out what your value is asking them at the end of a session. "What did you find most valuable today?" or "What is your biggest takeaway from our session?"

By doing this, you will receive an immediate response to that particular session verses the broad scope. It is also more top of mind for the client since they haven't had time to forget. Plus, it will cement the learning for them.

Mistake #3: Deceptions, White Lies, and Stretching the Truth

Many small business owners and entrepreneurs mentioned that honesty was an important element of their success. During the recession in 2008, the fact that they were ethical in their practices was the determining factor that kept their businesses afloat.

Honesty seems like it should be a given, but a lot of industries reported that honesty wasn't a common practice and had a surprising ripple effect. My interviewees revealed that the dishonesty of others in their field made it hard for the honest ones to be trusted and they had to work harder to gain that trust. But, on the flip side, they reported that once the owner earned the reputation for being honest, building up their business was much easier.

Devious Practices Hurt Industries at Large

According to the Consumer Culture Report in 2020, 71 percent of consumers consider the values of a company before making a purchase. What companies do matters, and it has an effect how consumers look at various industries at large.[14]

For example, in the coaching industry, a common practice is for someone to grow tired of the day job and decide that telling people what to do with their life would be a great way to make a living. Some even go as far as deciding that they are going to teach people how to become rich or some other thing that they have no experience doing.

This practice causes harm. I witnessed a self-proclaimed coach give advise to an abuse victim that could have easily gotten the victim killed and was in direct violation of the local city laws. That self-proclaimed coach had no experience with domestic violence and no training. Other common mistakes coaches do are to put up the shingle and claim to be an expert in health or nutrition when they had gone on a health journey

---

[14] "Ethical Dilemmas: How Scandals Damage Companies." March 2, 2021. www.wgu.edu/blog/ethical-dilemmas-how-scandals-damage-companies1909.html.

themselves. The problem with this is the coach oftentimes only teaches what worked for them. These individuals have no knowledge about the various other health challenges and issues that may be at play, and they are not doctors. It is not only unethical to do this kind of work, but it is also dangerous for everyone involved.

These kinds of practices make it harder for other coaches who have a wealth of experience and education to be taken seriously. It hurts the industry and is one of the reasons there have been movements for coaches to be required to become licensed. It is also a huge contributing factor to why other health care practitioners have resentment toward coaches and resistance in creating collaborations. These types of stories and issues are found in every industry, for example, the widespread bank corruption in the financial world and Theranos in the healthcare technology world.

Cutting corners and other dishonest practices hurts an industry as a whole and leads to more regulations and restrictions.

The Long-Term Effects of Showing Up and Other Commitments

Besides the more obvious deceptions in everyday practice of doing business, there are more subtle deceptions that can also affect your experience as an entrepreneur. A common one is not doing what you say you will do. Many people think showing up to a business meeting late is not that big of a deal. Nor do they worry about being days late sending an e-mail or forgetting about calling when they said they would. When they don't do what they say they will, people notice. This reflects poorly on the entire business, not to mention the individual.

Ivan Misner, the president of BNI (Business Network International), a global networking association, did a study on how showing up to the networking group affected the number of referrals passed. In that association, each member makes a commitment to show up weekly. He found the chapters that had the fewest absences closed the most business. In fact, when one group reduced the absences by 50 percent the referrals went up 71 percent.[15] This finding underlies just how important showing up is for getting business.

---

[15] I. Misner. September 27, 2021. "Show Up to Get More Referrals—Dr. Ivan Misner®." https://ivanmisner.com/show-up-to-get-more-referrals/.

If something comes up that makes it challenging to do what you say you will do, the best policy is to be upfront about the delays and inform the other party.

Being Late and Other Questionable Practices

According to a survey done by ABC News, 15 to 20 percent of the United States population arrives late to work. They report this widespread tardiness causes $90 billion loss in productivity. Not only does lateness hurts companies revenue, but it also affects how the business is perceived.[16]

Many people view those who are late as rude and unorganized and as someone they can't completely trust. Oftentimes people are late because they don't pay attention to the clock. They often move from doing one thing to the next without realizing that the time has passed. To stop being late, implementing structure often helps. Setting alarms or putting in other reminders can be helpful.

There is a lot of argument that these continually late people are optimistic and believe they can accomplish one more thing. This type of individual underestimates how much they can achieve in a certain amount of time. A good strategy to counter that tendency is, if possible, bringing that one more thing to the upcoming appointment. If you arrive early, do that one more thing while you wait.

Other people have a hard time calculating what time they should be in the car to arrive on time. The solution is to slip into a habit of figuring out how long it takes to arrive somewhere plus adding for the possibility of traffic, road construction, or accidents.

Being constantly late can cause a lot of long-term regret. People do not like waiting around and will eventually become frustrated or resentful that their time is not being respected. One of my clients had such a problem with being late that his business partner ended the relationship so he wouldn't have to deal with it anymore. That extreme shows how much damage can happen to your business. If you can't show up on time, it's a strong negative signal of how well you perform other parts of your business.

---

[16] "Running Late and Wasting Billions—ABC News." March 3, 2007. https://abcnews.go.com/.

One of the companies interviewed made it a policy to only hire people who show up on time, all the time. They emphasize that when the team members show respect for the company time, it makes it easier for the company to show respect for family time. They called it "respecting the yin and the yang of work life balance."

These are all places where honesty is not necessarily easy but important and builds trust. We all know in business that there are times when you don't want to necessarily tell the other person everything. That is fine, but don't purposely mislead someone, sooner or later, that will come back and bite.

The Problem With Trusting

Another issue that the entrepreneurs I interviewed made was trusting other people and vetting the people they bring into the company. Each person should prove they are trustworthy. One person interviewed went as far as building out systems that makes everything transparent, in effort to remove any dark corners. For example, both him and his business partner have access to all the information for bank accounts and all the documents so they don't need to just trust, but they can also verify.

Solopreneurs were also guilty of not protecting themselves from the dishonesty of others. Highly successful business strategist Stephanie Marie Beeby tells of her experience:

> Being an entrepreneur is a journey of discovering who you are and an act of being of service. The balance of knowing how to take care of yourself and how to meet the needs of others is a delicate one. One of the earliest mistakes and hardest lessons to learn was in my first career in real estate. I was only 21 and putting myself through college by selling homes.
>
> A fellow independent agent who worked with me in an office was getting married and leaving on a two-month European vacation. She asked me to watch over her real estate deals and manage her customers while she was gone in exchange for paying me a percentage of the commission. I excitedly accepted.

While she was gone, I did such a good job that everyone at the meeting mentioned several times how I knew more about the deals than the original agent. Three months later when the homes were closing, I notice I wasn't getting paid the commission I was promised. I talked with our sales manager about it. He wasn't aware of such an agreement and the other agent denied making the deal. Without a contract there was nothing he could do.

This wasn't some random person off the street stealing from me. It was a family friend and colleague that had known me since I was barely a preteen. When I approached her about it, she leaned in and whispered, "You are young. You will make it up."

It was at that moment I learned to get everything in writing, regardless of your relationship. That error cost me over $35,000, but I never made the same mistake again, and I have helped many clients to avoid it too.

—Stephanie Marie Beeby, Consultant and Strategist

The need for contracts is critical in today's environment. The price of not having one can cost the entrepreneur money, like Beeby found out, and it can also cost friends and business and create a lot of headaches.

Contracts help each party to define and know what is expected of each other. They protect the interests of the parties. A good contract also addresses how certain issues will be handled if a situation arises. It also provides legal protection for all parties involved if done correctly.

Application Corner

Exercise: Honesty Check

Here are some places to look at for honesty:

- Do you do the things that you said you are going to do, when you said that you are going to do them?
- Do you withhold information to make people think one thing, but the truth is actually another?

Resources

Holtzclaw, E. n.d. "6 Ways Dishonesty Can Actually Save Your Business | Inc
.Com." www.inc.com/eric-holtzclaw/believe-me-lying-works-how-dishonesty-
can-save-your-company.html (accessed May 5, 2022).

Kawasaki, G. January 2001. "The Top Ten Lies of Entrepreneurs." https://hbr
.org/2001/01/the-top-ten-lies-of-entrepreneurs.

Mistake #4: Refuses to Take Risks

Some people love risk. Some people hate it. Some have a confusing relationship with it. But when it boils down to being a business owner and entrepreneur, the job is all about risks. You will win with some. You will lose with some. There is no way to determine which one will be the winner. The market is a fickle place. The smallest detail strays off, and boom, things flop. Other times, for no apparent reason, the business takes off. Michael Porter, a Harvard Professor, has a theory that there are five forces that will impact success in business. He considers the competition in the industry, how easy is it to get in business, suppliers strength, customer influence, and the how high the threat exist with being replaced by other products.[17]

Sometimes this risk, and the fear of losing what someone already has, will hold a person back, which doesn't work. Richard MacDonald, a successful nitro engine builder, said not taking enough risk was his biggest holdback when launching his business. He describes the challenge of risk-taking and the struggle he had with it.

The biggest mistake I made in my nitro engine business was not buying enough equipment when I had the money. If I would have had those machines, it could have compelled me further with a lot less bumps. I reached a point where I needed the equipment to meet the work demand to have the capability as a machine shop owner to be competitive.

It is a tricky balance between the acquisition of the equipment relative to the accumulation of income. If I think the machine won't bring in the income, I don't purchase it, and I become stagnant

There is also a psychological factor in this because if I don't solve the problem of being able to replace myself at my level of craft, the investment in the equipment becomes a trap because of the lack of manpower.

---

[17] M.E. Porter. November 4, 2009. "Competitive Strategy: Techniques for Analyzing Industries and Competitors," *Papers* (SSRN). https://papers.ssrn.com/sol3/papers.cfm?abstract_id=1496175.

If I was to go back, I would have sought the insight of a knowledgeable accountant to help me better judge the profit loss ratio. Also uncover what tax ramifications there would be. I would have searched for more effective ways to replace myself or better ways to train someone to a helpful level so I could grow as a business and not be limited to my own capacity.

—Richard C. MacDonald, Nitro Engine Builder

In his statement, we can see that MacDonald regretted not taking a bigger risk. After years of reflection, he realized that tapping into the resources of a skilled entrepreneur accountant and receiving better guidance would have empowered him to take the risk that he now regrets not taking.

The only way to really win big is to take risks. Thoughtful, calculated, measured steps. We're not talking about the rent money on the roulette table, but risks that seem like good calculations, and see what goes right. In order to not take too much risk, it is important to establish decision-making guardrails. These guardrails that you put up in your business are to assist you from unintentionally driving off into dangerous territory.

Naturally, the guardrails will differ widely from business to business depending on the circumstances, how many people are in the company, the risk tolerance, and the nature of the business.

Some of my guardrails I have implemented in my own business:

- Never invest more than I can afford to lose.
- When doing a promotion, don't stop other activities that fill my funnel of prospects and don't count on the promotion to work first or second time out.
- Back up all important information.
- I have a set amount of time to figure out a new way of doing business.
- If my intuition is telling me something isn't right listen to my hunch.
- Track my numbers and don't guess if an effort is working. Look at the numbers.

The objective of guardrails isn't to stop failure and mistakes from happening because that is a natural part of business. The guardrails purpose is to make it possible for the business owner to be able to bounce back quickly when things don't work.

I also haven't met a business owner who took risks and failed that didn't come out of it without more knowledge. Sometimes, the only good thing that came out of the failure is experience and knowing what not to do.

Failure is a test to see how much you really want it. Are you willing to show what you are made of? Do you have the determination to pick yourself up and go for it again? Yes, failure sucks, and sometimes, it can have negative results, but it will lead you somewhere.

My personal philosophy is when one thing on top of another goes wrong, there are only so many things that can go wrong before the probability of something going right. I know it is a fallacy, but I still like to believe that it's true.

When I slip in one of those "everything is not working" modes, I become curious what will go right? Maybe it will be A or B? Then I create a wish list of what things I want to go right. Oftentimes, the thing that goes right is much better than I hoped.

What I am doing is making the risk appear less intense by making it my work game. By gamifying my task, I am taking the edge off. Gamification has become a buzz word in many business circles. Basically, what it means is to take elements of a game and apply it to your business.

The way it is applied now started taking root in 2010. The principles of celebrating a person taking action in business through badges, awards, and tracking progress have been used well by the most popular social media platforms.[18] Or in my case through just making my business more fun even if I am only competing against myself. In the words of Lisa Jones, a gamification expert:

The positive aspect of gamification for entrepreneurs is that their target audience is more apt to "buy in" to their concept and try it if it is a game. The best way to set it up is as a friendly competition, so

---

[18] H. Chitroda. June 4, 2015. "A Brief History on Gamification." https://knolskape .com/brief-history-gamification/.

that participants want to be involved to join in the fun. There are ways to make it so that the stakes are low, and there aren't any negative consequences.

The flip side of gamification is that not everyone will want to be involved. There are ways to gain "buy-in," but it isn't always easy, and it takes forethought and strategy. The most important part of gamification, though, is to have participants feel motivated to want to join in, and not feel forced.

—Lisa Jones, Professional Speaker and Gamification Expert

Stopping the Success Train

Another challenge business owners talked about was fear of losing what they had gained. When you have already achieved some success, it is easy to slip into this and shift into a pattern of playing it safe. Determining if you are doing this requires studying at what you are doing and why you are doing it.

Part of the problem is many entrepreneurs, small business owners, freelancers, and solopreneurs don't see themselves as CEOs, when in fact that is exactly what they are. A CEO is the primary person responsible for making the decisions and making sure the company is profitable.

The CEOs' duties vary from company to company, but ultimately, they are the ones who are supposed to make sure the company's operations are working. Often, they are in charge of the culture too. They are the leader of the business even if it is only one person.

According to the research Harvard conducted, rookie CEOs are outperforming experienced executives in taking their companies to higher markets and are experiencing less fluctuation with stock prices.

What aspect of risk-taking are these first-time CEOs using that those with more life experience are not? The research suggests that inexperienced CEOs are applying more curiosity and more willingness to take risks. Curiosity is making these rookies more adaptable and more flexible, giving them the ability to confront problems with fresh eyes rather than being constrained by how they have always done it.[19]

---

[19] T. Bower. January 1, 2021. "Why Rookie CEOS Outperform Experienced Executives Rely Too Much on Old Playbooks," *Harvard Business Review.* https://hbr.org/2021/01/why-rookie-ceos-outperform.

Doing things the same way can have adverse effects. The world is changing, and the old ways might keep you trapped with diminishing returns.

Acting Like a CEO

When my oldest was about eleven months old, one of her favorite things to do was to ask me the question, "What's that? What's that? What's that?"

Once she had worn out her investigation in the trailer we lived in, she would start screaming, "Outside, outside, outside."

As soon as we went outside, with everything she saw, she kicked into the repetitive question again, "What's that? What's that?"

Thank heavens, my other children weren't like that!

But after reading Adam Bryant's article, "How to Think Like a CEO," at strategy-business.com, I thought maybe it wouldn't have been so bad if my other children would have been obsessed with understanding everything.

Adam Bryant conducted in-depth interviews with more than 500 CEOs. He was trying to discover what put that individual into the top position. He found that most CEOs did not fit the stereotype people have of what a CEO is like. He claimed that there was no defining factor of sex, age, ethnic group, or company size.

Only one thing, he found, was the defining factor that dominated every CEO: applied curiosity, which he argues is used when people question over and over again in pursuit of understanding.[20]

In the same way, my daughter was relentless in understanding the world and figuring out everything about it, CEOs do this in their business. They are relentless in understanding how things work. And once they discover how things function, they become relentless in figuring out the patterns and insights from that to question everything they know.

This questioning and probing gives them the competitive advantage and guides them to take risks in a calculated way.

---

[20] A. Bryant. October 15, 2019. "How to Think Like a CEO." www.strategy business.com/blog/How-to-think-like-a-CEO.

Applied Curiosity Training

The good news: applied curiosity can be built. So my other children can develop the muscle that wasn't so natural for them, and so can you and I too.

Where to begin?

A possible place to develop this habit is in your CEO meeting. This meeting doesn't require you to have staff. You can have it with just yourself. It's helpful to have a weekly CEO meeting and ask questions about the patterns and insights you see in your performance over the week, trends you are seeing with your clients, and everything you became aware of in your field.

One area I recommend entrepreneurs look at is their focus. I suggest they check in with their objectives and consider how they are progressing forward on their quarterly milestones. After this, they can examine the best next step to move forward. (Don't forget to look at the mindset you need to achieve it too.)

Another way to gain perspective is to bring in some outside eyes who have no bias about what you are doing and that only want your best interest. We often get too close to the subject and can't see things as clearly as someone who has fresh eyes and no attachments and who has been trained to see the patterns. A third party with the skills to understand who you are and what you are about can ask questions that can completely transform your business in a positive way.

Application Corner

Exercise #1: Applied Curiosity to Your Risk

Identify a risk in your business you are considering taking.

Define the pros and cons.

If you were forced to be more curious about the various options, what other considerations would you look into?

Who could you talk to gain more understanding?

What question have you not asked about this risk yet?

Is there a way you could limit the exposure?

Is there another option you haven't considered?

Exercise #2: Gamifying Your Risk

What was your favorite game you played when you were a child?

What elements of that game made it fun for you?

How can you apply those elements to your current work?

What reward system can you put in place to make risk-taking fun and results-driven?

CHAPTER 2

Neglecting to Do One's Homework: Unprepared, Not Competitive, and Failing to Know What Will Be on the Exam

My path to being an entrepreneur was unexpected. As a young adult, I was one of those people who smugly ignored all those boring business books at the bookstore, knowing that I would never need to read them. Now I shoot to read a business book a week and wish I had more time to consume all the knowledge.

At the time, my dreams were consumed with being a bestselling fiction author who had nothing to do with business. After publishing my first book and working with the publisher on promotion, I learned that by neglecting the fundamentals of sales and marketing, I had done myself a big disservice. I had to play catch up, competing against people who knew what they were doing.

The nature of business underlies all of life. We are always selling and marketing as part of living with one another. Business at its core is providing a product or service that helps others, making the world go around. The more we understand the nature of business, the better our service or product will be.

Mistake #5: Didn't Stay on Top of Their Industry

Seventy-two percent of the business owners I interviewed mentioned that they wished they had known either more about their industry when they started or how important it is for them to stay on top of the industry.

This ranges from staying abreast of the latest technology and knowing where your industry is headed to leaping in front of the pack.

One business owner mentioned how he had a solid system of tracking his sales. It wasn't hard for him to see when traditional advertising was no longer working. Most of his work came from traditional means. He knew almost immediately when the shift happened from watching his numbers. He even pushed it as far as to put out a traditional ad that said he would pay people money just for giving him a phone call. No one called. By keeping tabs on his field and what was working, he made the shift with the trends without many headaches, which kept him in business when the recession hit. In contrast, a lot of his competitors went out of business.

Another small business owner admitted that he wasn't paying much attention to the changes in his field. He put his energy into finishing the work in front of him. He laughed as he confessed that if he kept ignoring industry changes, he would fall way behind. He knew if he didn't make a shift in his behavior soon, it would impact his income.

Before the crash happened in 2008, I was a life coach. The stock market took its dive, and the next day, I woke up as a business coach. It was clear from the phone calls that day my clients no longer cared about whether their lives were fulfilling or they were getting along with their spouses. Their top concern became how they were going to put food on the table and deal with the emotional impact of the stock market crash.

Another major shift happened quickly when COVID-19 spread across the world. Those who fared better during the pandemic either had businesses that could meet the need that the pandemic created—food delivery services, cleaning services, online companies, and the like—or those who made unique adaptations to the situation. That is not to say every company would survive, but those who were in the service industry and used creativity to meet their customers' needs did have a higher chance of survival.[1]

Having the flexibility to adjust your work and services to your ideal client's needs and to global reality is critical for your company's success.

---

[1] R. Arora. June 30, 2020. "Which Companies Did Well During the Coronavirus Pandemic?," *Forbes.* www.forbes.com/sites/rohitarora/2020/06/30/which-companies-did-well- during-the-coronavirus-pandemic/.

A business owner needs to stay on top of what their client wants. This includes knowing the best way to be in front of their prospects.

During the COVID storm, many thought leaders were tracking the overall psychology of their clients and potential clients. They paid attention to the emotional shifts occurring. They knew when it first started; the pandemic gave a global shock. People weren't buying because of widespread unemployment, and customers cut back spending. People weren't ready to hear most business offerings. Those who did market and promote at the time often came across as not being sensitive to what was happening and rarely did a promotion do well.[2]

Then a massive wave of companies and businesses responded by offering free or inexpensive training online. During that surge, I, along with many others, took advantage of opportunities that wouldn't have been available under different circumstances. It was a mass surplus of people worldwide doing what they could to support others.

Of course, companies aren't in business to do things for free, and quickly, they couldn't sustain it, and there was a global outcry of Zoom fatigue. People didn't want to be in front of their computers anymore, and they were tired of trainings and staying home. They were tired of the social injustice continuing to happen. And they certainly didn't ever want to hear the word COVID again. Businesses were going through their own struggles, needing more income. Hence, all sorts of weird price hikes penetrated the market.

And on and on went the waves, hitting almost every sector. People had spent too much time at home and with that time realized their job wasn't working for them. Corporate and small businesses started experiencing the Great Resignation. They panicked to fill the empty positions and took whoever showed up with little vetting, which in turn resulted in lost money from hiring the wrong person. That, in turn, created a new way of hiring to access prospects in a way that hopefully avoided that mistake but became incredibly time-consuming for the job hunter requiring them to go through multiple rounds of assessment and interviews.

---

[2] A. Di Crosta, I. Ceccato, and D. Marchettie. August 16, 2021. "Psychological Factors and Consumer Behavior During the COVID-19," Plos.org. https://journals.plos.org/plosone/article?id=10.1371/journal.pone.0256095.

If the business owner wasn't tracking these reactions to the global events, they wouldn't make the most informed decisions.

One Method of Keeping on Top of Your Industry

According to the article, "Most CEOs Read a Book A Week. This Is How You Can Too" by Jim Kwik, most CEOs read a book a week.[3] The practice of accumulating knowledge through regular reading can be a game changer in your business if you apply the relevant information. It gives you leverage for many reasons.

1. Keeps you current on your industry, especially if you read industry journals and newspapers.
2. Develop a deeper understanding of your topic. One way is to read your industry's foundational books, the most bestselling in your area of focus, and a recently published book on that subject. This will give you a broad understanding of the important issues on the topic and what is the current conversation.
3. Gain an understanding of your expertise in the field.
4. Keep innovating.
5. Broaden your exposure to others' thinking.
6. Pick up on themes and various arguments to make more informed decisions.
7. Enhance your creativity.
8. Lessen your bias.
9. Increase your thought processes and deepen your understanding of structure.

When I taught freshman composition, I became fascinated why some of my students seemed to intuitively understand the structure of a good rhetorical essay and others did not. The first thing that I looked at was

---

[3] B.D. Evans. June 27, 2017. "Most CEOS Read a Book a Week. This Is How You Can Too (According to This Renowned Brain Coach)," *Inc.* www.inc.com/brian-d-evans/most-ceos-read-a-book-a-week-this-is-how-you-can-too-according-to-this-renowned-.html.

the school districts the students came from. The district certainly made a difference in their level of writing since some students had access to more resources and higher levels of instruction.

Also, a lot of research has been done proving that if the student wrote about something they were passionate about, their level of writing improved.[4] As more students poured through my classrooms, I monitored my statistic of who did well in class and which students dropped out or struggled. And I found that the school districts they came from did matter, but some students from the lower-ranked school districts also did well.

The more I delved into why some students understood structure, the clearer it became there was one thing that made the biggest difference. The avid readers understood the logical flow better than those who self-reported reading rarely.

Then I added reading exercises to class; we would read and dissect an article and explore how an essay was put together. Lo and behold, the students' ability to form an argument improved. Reading strengthens a person's ability to engage in critical thinking. A key element to being on top of your industry is critical thinking, which leads to better decision making and business operations.

Some Possible Approaches to Stay on Top of Your Industry

- **Join the top association in your industry**. You can find value and many resources in professional associations. They often provide monthly training on relevant topics that help you build business. They also provide access to resources and vetted services. Associations connect you with peers and future mentors. Active participation benefits also include cross promotions, support, and friendships, in addition to understanding your industry better.
- **Read annual industry reports.** These reports offer timely information on a broad scope of industry trends. They give a general sense of where the industry is heading for the next

---

[4] K. Bain. 2004. *What the Best College Teachers Do* (Harvard University Press).

year. Most often, they include sections on how to adapt and
use the information.

- **Subscribe to leading newspapers and magazines.** Scanning
the leading newspapers and magazines monthly will give
you an idea of the kinds of subjects that are in the news, the
type of issues the industry is concerned about, and what is
top of mind for some leaders. This kind of information will
empower you and give you industry language and raise your
awareness of the innovation being explored.

- **Study your competition.** Whether you visit their brick-and-
mortar site or their website, you can learn a lot about how
your competition is operating. Many successful businesses
have resulted from studying their competition and determining what they are not addressing or how to provide better
service or the product more cost-effective.

- One caveat: don't base your business practices on what you see
on the surface of another business. A business strategy that works
for a leading expert might not be the best approach for you. You
might not have the platform they have to be successful with their
approach. Also, you probably don't have enough information
about why they are doing a particular business practice. Some of
the bigger companies are able to run at a loss to gain marketing
information they can use on the backend to make a profit. Some
of what you see might be designed to run at a loss.

- **Follow your industry's leading thought leaders.** Most
industries have a well-known thought leader or leaders who
track what is going on in the industry and transform the
information into digestible chunks. Follow their YouTube chan-
nel, sign up for their podcast, subscribe to their newsletters, to
stay on top of bite-size information pertinent to your business.

Application Corner

Exercise: #1 Industry Trends

List 10 things that are changing in your industry.
After you have the list, write down the ways you plan to prepare for
the changes.

Exercise: #2 Spot Check

What are the current emotions your customers are currently feeling?

How are these emotions showing up in their buying behavior?

How are these emotions showing up in their response to different types of marketing?

How can your product or services best meet your clients' emotional needs right now?

Exercise #3: Battle Plan to Stay on Top of the Industry

Review the aforementioned list.

Add any other ideas you have to stay on top of your industry I might have missed.

Pick one or two of those activities and come up with a strategy for how you are going to apply that activity at least monthly.

Mistake #6: Didn't Look to the Future

A successful businesswoman was the envy of many in her field and had all the work that she wanted without advertising. People flocked to her by referrals. Her current clientele was loyal and did not want to go anywhere else.

When I interviewed her, though, she was having huge regret about how she ran her business. It wasn't the work itself. She loved that. What she regretted was that she hadn't set herself up for the future. She was getting close to retirement age, but her business was built on the time-in time-out model, and she didn't have enough savings to support her not working. There was no leeway or structure in her business for retirement or even to work fewer hours without impacting her current lifestyle.

Years earlier, she had thought about bringing someone else onto her team to learn the craft, her methods, and the things that made her successful and do a profit-split agreement, but she never got around to it.

Because she didn't bring anyone on board at that time, she is now faced with having to work and has no one with her qualifications to refer her clients to when she becomes tired or has to quit because of increasing health issues.

She regretted not giving herself the ability to make money without having to do the physical work. Even though it would have taken more effort and focus on scaling her business out of the time-in time-out model—she would have been better setup for retirement.

Now, she is forced to either keep working and forget retirement or put the structures in place currently. She expressed concern about scaling her business as her energy and physical ability were waning. A good resource for someone in this type of situation would be book *E-Myth Revisited* by Michael Gerber.

In the Forbes article, "As CEO You're the Futurist of Your Business," Jim Blasigame makes the argument that if you are heading your business, you are the futurist of your company. The entrepreneur makes plans and then goes through the process of bringing that plan into the marketplace.[5]

---

[5] J. Blasingame. August 27, 2017. "As CEO, You're the Futurist of Your Business." www.forbes.com/. www.forbes.com/sites/jimblasingame/2017/08/27/as-ceo-youre-the-futurist-of-your-business/?sh=4d251ace795e.

What futurists do is watch and analyze emerging patterns. For the entrepreneur, the focus would be on the patterns and circumstances that are happening with their clients to better predict their upcoming needs and address those needs so they can better serve them.

The state of the industry reports mentioned earlier is helpful in uncovering the overall trends and factors that are affecting business. Many come out at the beginning of the year and typically will uncover emerging trends that will be important to keep an eye on.

In my business, I listen for what emerges out of my coaching sessions. If three clients in one day express a common mood, attitude, or struggle, I pay attention and research if there is an emerging pattern and, if so, what is causing the common concerns and emotions.

Putting All Eggs in One Basket and Not Prepared for the Changing of the Rules (i.e., Facebook, Amazon, and the Government)

A common mistake entrepreneurs make is to have an overreliance on any one platform to communicate with their clients and prospects. The more that the entrepreneur can maintain control of their ability to communicate, the better able they will be to weather unexpected storms.

One of my colleagues was an extremely successful science fiction author. He was making six figures writing a series and selling the books on a popular social media site by using direct messaging bots. That particular site changed the rules of how the direct message could be used, and overnight, he was no longer able to communicate with his buying public. His business dried up.

A similar thing happened to another colleague of mine who wrote thrillers. He went from making thousands of dollars a day to losing thousands of dollars with an unannounced change of rules on Amazon. I have colleagues who have been blocked out of their main social media account for no apparent reason. They lost contact with all their prospects. These stories can go on and on and underline the risk of being an online business.

My colleagues, who knew the risk of working with these platforms and took measures and strategies to move these prospects onto their own mail lists and/or have other ways of contacting their prospects and clients, faired a lot better when these untimely but expected changes of rules happened.

Other remedies to this problem are to clearly understand who your consumer is and what marketing messages resonate with them, marketing channels can wax and wane with effectiveness, but as long as you know the core of how to talk effectively to your consumer, you can find new avenues of reaching them. Plus, keep diversified set of marketing channels including working on some of your own.

Didn't Think Big Enough

One entrepreneur admitted that his biggest mistake was not thinking big enough when he started his business. When he began his company, his total focus was on the local market. He never considered that his business might thrive and expand nationally.

By not thinking big enough about the possibilities, he never took the time to trademark his business name. Another extremely well-known national company had the same name as his. Consumers confused the two companies for years until the other national company with the same name bought him out.

Not thinking big enough issue not only relates to trademarking. Oftentimes, not thinking big enough shows up in the preplanning, launching, and execution in business. Looking for ways you can add a little extra and standout can have a huge payoff.

In order to truly think big being in an abundance mindset is critical. If we as business owners are focused on what we get out of everything we do, it will tamper the way we show up in business.

I personally know a thought leader who built high multimillion dollar business through her radical gift giving. She enjoys giving her prospects books, pens, and calendars to add value to her prospects. Focusing more on what she can give not only paid off financially but also paid in good will she built.

Didn't Realize How Volatile Business Would Be

Several small business owners and entrepreneurs mentioned that for years getting business and making sales had been easy for them. They made the mistake of thinking it would stay that way. When the recession hit and other global events changed the business environment, they were not prepared for a suddenly rocky road. Turbulence is not the exception; eventually, harder times come. To prepare for this, expect it will come. Plan for it. If possible, put money aside so you have a buffer and reserves for hard times and can take advantage of opportunities.

When the hard times come, limit the reminiscing about good times and focus on what needs to be done. Opportunities will present themselves during the challenge. Huge insights, competitive advantages, plus personal and company growth can result from tough times.

Also, let others' horror stories be a warning. If they grow their business on a fad or trend, there is an unknown expiration date. The closer you are to solving a fundamental human need, the more enduring your business can be. Be prepared that bumps will come and set plans in place to absorb the downturn.

Soft Skills Are the Future

In higher education, a common topic among educators is empowering students with the knowledge of the discipline and in the workforce.[6] A growing amount of research is finding that in order for students to compete in the global work environment, they need both tech skills and soft skills. The LinkedIn Global Talent Trend reported that 92 percent of employers ranked soft skills higher than tech skills.[7]

Soft skills are people skills such as communication, listening, and conflict management. This includes critical thinking, creativity, and the ability to perform at ones best. Businesses have found employees who have these skills do better in the workplace.

---

[6] A. Doyle. February 21, 2021. "What Are Soft Skills?: Definition and Examples of Soft Skills." www.thebalancecareers.com/. www.thebalancecareers.com/what-are-soft-skills-2060852.

[7] "LinkedIn Releases 2019 Global Talent Trends Report." January 28, 2019. https://news.linkedin.com/. https://news.linkedin.com/2019/January/linkedin-releases-2019-global-talent-trends-Report.

According to Ottawa University, the top skills employers are looking for in 2022 are adaptability, communication, time management, emotional intelligence, leadership, and critical thinking.[8]

The topic of soft skills and the need to have them doesn't look like it will be going away anytime soon.[9]

Prepared for Criticism and Mean People

Several entrepreneurs interviewed mentioned that they were not prepared for the emotional ride that being in business would have. They were not ready for the people being mean and the amount of criticism that was lobbied at them from face-to-face interactions, online reviews, and especially with social media comments.

It is almost impossible to avoid haters, criticizers, and receiving negative backlash when in pursuit of doing good. It is important to develop resiliency skills to bounce back or shake off hurtful actions.[10]

An entrepreneur does better if they realize that not everyone is going to love what they are up to. In fact, it is preferred that not everyone approves. When you throw a rock in the river, there is a ripple effect. Having people disagree with what you are doing signifies you are on the right path. If there isn't any resistance to your efforts, it might be a sign that you aren't differentiated enough.

Shifting to the Changing Environment

Others mentioned that they didn't realize the challenge that they would have keeping their business going in the midst of unexpected crisis in

---

[8] "10 Best Accounting Skills | Ottawa University." January 1, 2022. www.ottawa .edu/. www.ottawa.edu/online-and-evening/blog/july-2021/10-best-accounting-skills.

[9] S. A. Dean and J.I. East. 2019. "Soft Skills Needed for the 21st-Century Workforce." https://scholarworks.waldenu.edu/. https://scholarworks.waldenu.edu/cgi/viewcontent.cgi?article=1260&context=ijamt.

[10] "How to Handle Hates." August 16, 2021. https://startuphustle.xyz/. https://startuphustle.xyz/blog/how-to-deal-with-haters/.

their personal life. Such events like death, divorce, and illness make it challenging to stay in business. This, too, requires an increased amount of resiliency skills to balance both demands. This is another good reason to put processes in your business.

According to the data collected from more than 500 entrepreneurs in the United States, Amanda Bullough and Maija Renko found that the entrepreneurs' belief in their ability and resiliency traits was critical during hard times.

In their findings, the best way to ride the waves of challenge was first for the entrepreneur to be trained in business development to the point the entrepreneur was confident in their abilities. The second was to connect through networking and mentorship with other more seasoned entrepreneurs. This gives the entrepreneur the chance to witness resiliency traits in action. And, thirdly, for the entrepreneur to be in the game of growing their business, so they can receive immediate feedback from the market and from those who can be objective, encouraging, and offer con-structive evaluation.[11]

Preparing for the future is a multifaceted endeavor from forecast-ing and making sure that the business model is supportive for upcom-ing events like retirement. It also entails positioning the business to best handle the unexpected growth. But probably the most important aspects of preparing for the future are developing and enhancing soft skills and building resiliency to handle any curve ball.

Application Corner

Exercise #1: Planning for the Future

- Is your current business model the one you want to be doing in 5, 10, or 20 years from now?
- If not, what can you do now to prepare for the option of retirement?
- Do you need to bring on someone else?

---

[11] A. Bullough and M. Renko. 2013. "Entrepreneurial Resilience During Challenging Times," *Business Horizons* 56, no. 3, pp. 343–350.

- Do you have another passive income stream that you can put in place?
- Do you have a policy and procedure manual so that others can follow your system?
- Do you need to create training videos so others can learn your system easily?
- Do you have a solid plan for retirement? How does your business play into that? What targets does it need to hit in terms of profitability, revenue, and delegation to meet your goals?

Exercise #2: Fire Drill for Your Business

A good way to evaluate your current business operation is to assess what needs to be in place if you were to go to the hospital, enjoy a vacation, or otherwise take time off and still have the business function without hiccups.

At this moment, how well would your business function without you?

If it is anything less than absolutely great, what needs to be put in place for it to run smoothly?

Exercise #3: Hard Times Preparation

List what possible hard times could be heading your way based on history of your industry.

Example:

- Economic downturns
- Seasonal sells
- Risk of new competition
- Change in political leadership that affects grants, regulations, government funding, and so on.
- Supply chain issues, and so forth.

List actions to take and possible strategies to put in place to prepare for hard times.

If you are in a hard time, what do you need to do to weather the storm and remember to think big and look for the possibilities.

Resources

Brodsky, M. 2011. "Sustainable Survival in a Volatile Economy—Wharton Magazine." https://magazine.wharton.upenn.edu/. https://magazine.wharton .upenn.edu/issues/fall- 2011/sustainable-survival-in-a-volatile-economy/.

Ungar, M., L. Theron, K. Murphy, and P. Jefferies. January 12, 2021. "Researching Multisystemic Resilience: Sample Methodology." www.frontiersin.org/. www .frontiersin.org/articles/10.3389/fpsyg.2020.607994/full.

Mistake #7: Unprepared for the Time, Cost, and Loneliness Involved

Many owners and entrepreneurs stated they were unprepared for the work, time, and cost required to be successful. For example, one person was stuck in corporate, feeling like their life was being sucked out of them. All they could dream about was breaking away from their corporate job and going it alone. They were filled with dreams about how wonderful it would be to be their own boss, do what they love, set their own schedule, and keep most of the money. When this person did break loose, they were shocked and disenchanted by the reality.

The idea of being an entrepreneur has been romanticized with visions of being one's own boss, having one's own schedule, and having no limit to the money that can be made. Often entrepreneurs start out by thinking they are good at something, so why not go into business doing that?

Most entrepreneurs are motivated by higher goals than just money. Some want to be able to meet family commitments. Others are driven to improve the world. Some have been obsessed to do entrepreneurial pursuits from early childhood. But the reality is doing the work that you love is only a small part of the picture. At the core of the business is working on marketing, sales, financials, and dealing with tech issues, which are often not the entrepreneur's favorite tasks. It helps a lot to love the process of business because the reality of doing what it takes to be successful is a lot more than just doing the actual service.

According to Freshbooks, a new business takes between two and three years to cover the expense and around 7 to 10 years to be profitable.[12] Be prepared. Launching a business takes a lot of work. Running a business takes more work. Taking your business to the next level ramps up the work even more. As mentioned before, being an entrepreneur is about taking risks regularly: betting on yourself, your idea, your skills, and on luck that you'll make it.

The nature of being an entrepreneur is not for those people who like a lot of safety, a guaranteed paycheck, and payment for all the efforts that

---

[12] "How Long It Takes for a Small Business to Be Successful: A Year-By-Year Breakdown." March 28, 2019. www.freshbooks.com/hub/startup/how-long-does-it-take-business-to-be-successful.

one puts out. The realization will come that clients most often don't just arrive on the doorstep when a shingle is hung up, declaring you open for business.

Often, there is an extended period of time when all the money goes back into the business. In fact, many business owners take out loans to get going or when they want to scale. That is the opposite of having money coming in and doesn't match the dream many people have when thinking about launching out on their own. It is helpful to think long term and be comfortable with the possibility of having less short term in order to have a better shot for the long term.

Then there is the fluctuation of inconsistent money. Their business doesn't have to stay that way. But until they have a deep understanding of their market, how to convert prospects into paying clients, and the most effective way to provide deliverables, there will be a time of unreliable cash flow. If a business is seasonally based, the reality might always be inconsistent.

The amount of time it takes to make a business successful can impact the entrepreneur's finances unless they have prepared for it. The person who jumps from corporate can find it shocking to go from being paid for time put in to many hours of unpaid work with the hope of bringing in money at some point. Many entrepreneurs who leave corporate life experience a dramatic pay decrease, which can put financial pressure on them that they are not used to. On the positive side, those who go through the entrepreneurial journey and embrace the struggle come out with a solid understanding of highly valuable skills such as management, leadership, sales, and marketing.

Time Schedule Freedom

A top desire of many entrepreneurs is to have the freedom to create their own time schedule, which is true, but not really. When I first started my business, I had recently gone through a divorce. The court ruled on a visitation schedule with the children. I thought one way to cope with the loss of not having the children all the time would be to work on the days I didn't have them and be with them the days that did.

In theory, that sounded great. In actuality, business doesn't work that way. I would make the phone calls on my workdays, and people would call me back on my non workdays. I would post available delivery days. Then, the potential client would have a schedule that didn't conform to that time frame. Plus, the business network meetings happened on my non workdays. On and on it went.

For the most part, I was able to schedule late afternoons and early evenings off, but then I would return to work after the children were in bed. Starting a business does require a lot of hours initially, with the hope and prayer that someday all this work will pay off financially.

Often, it is said to be an entrepreneur you work until the job is done, but the job is never really done. Many entrepreneurs work extremely long hours and put in more time than they would in a corporate job. The hours that an entrepreneur applies varies greatly. Many of the reasons depend on what stage they are at in their business. More hours are most likely not needed if they have the funnels and systems in place. The hours are also determined by how ambitious they are and how much money the entrepreneur wants to make.[13]

Fighting Isolation in the Workplace

A factor of being an entrepreneur that is rarely talked about is how lonely working for oneself can be. Regularly, the sole entrepreneur is on their own to make things happen. Rarely do their romantic partners or family and friends understand their business or the pressures they are under. As a result of this isolation, many entrepreneurs look for business partnerships but that can be problematic. Suppose an entrepreneur searches for a partner to do what they least like doing. Many times, that is to avoid doing those parts. That cheats them of understanding how each part of their business works. The CEO does need to understand how every part of their business works enough to manage it and see what a good person would be to fill that role.

---

[13] CBNation–Mercy. n.d. "20 Entrepreneurs Reveal How Much They Work in a Week." https://teach.ceoblognation.com/. https://teach.ceoblognation.com/2019/03/10/20-entrepreneurs-reveal-how-much-they-work-in-a-week/ (accessed April 21, 2022).

Time Management Woes

Another thing new entrepreneurs often struggle with is time management and knowing how to structure their day. They can become caught spending too much time on things that don't compel their business forward. To make matters worse, rarely is little space for a significant margin of error. The challenge for early entrepreneurs is knowing what is important. At the beginning, many people think everything is important, but as time goes on, it becomes more nuanced. For more experienced, it's not as much knowing what is important to spend time on but being able to get the time available in large enough chunks to make a real contribution. For more information, see Peter Drucker's book *Effective Executive.*

I work a lot with creative types of personality who cringe at the idea of being controlled by a calendar. For those types of people, which I am one of them, I advocate focusing more on developing routine and space to be able to enjoy flexibility in our work.

To do this, it does require discipline. There are things in business that must get done. The way I explain it is that every job has something about it that you won't like. So that being the case, figuring out how to do the stuff that you don't like with the least amount of pain is a good approach.

For example, one of the things I don't like doing is writing newsletters. I know, I am a writer, and it sounds like it would be something I like doing. Truthfully, I would much rather be writing a book. To minimize the process of writing a regular newsletter less painful, I chunk the work and write a whole bunch of newsletters at once.

My favorite way to do this when I lived in California was to drop my children off at school, drive down to the beach in the winter time, bring a fold out chair, sit on the beach, hearing the waves, and seeing the clouds, and write.

I made it a game. How many newsletters could I write before I had to leave to go pick up my children? The ocean waves calmed my nerves. The clouds and wind inspired me with ideas and the ticking clock kept me focused. By me thinking bigger on how to get something done, I had a day I looked forward to instead of dreaded.

Another thing I really don't like doing is taking what I call "money action steps." Money action steps can be anything from onboarding a client, paying bills, to cancelling unused subscriptions. Paying attention to our money is important. When we give our money love, it gives us love back. When we neglect it, less money comes into the business.

To make sure that I don't neglect money, I sign up online to do work sessions with other business owners. My commitment to myself and to my business is I will take any money action step that I need to do first in that session. For months, that meant I was on hold on the phone to deal with whatever money action step that was needed for most of the session. I of course did other small things while waiting on the phone.

No one likes being on hold for extended amount of time, but by me showing up on in those work sessions and addressing the money issues, I felt better the rest of the week. Not only did I feel better by doing this every week at a schedule time with public accountability, but my bank account reflected the extra effort.

What you don't like doing in your business might be different than my list. The trick is to figure out what it is. It is important to come up with a system that will make it less painful and will help you get it done.

Stifled by Not Understanding Time and Self-Improvement

The other part of time and entrepreneurship is understanding our relationship to time. Scientists are now uncovering how our emotions play into how we perceive time and how that connects to the task we are doing.

Mihaly Csikszentmihalyi was a pioneer in uncovering people's connection with time. His work centered around the concept of flow and how to shift into that state. When a person reaches a flow state, they are more motivated and have more desire for work. Further research has been done on how our emotions play a part in how we experience time. Negative emotions have the opposite effect on our motivation.[14]

When the emotions are positive, I would argue that our connection to time and our work is more positive and motivating. And when the work

---

[14] J. Dawson and S. Sleek. September 28, 2018. "The Fluidity of Time: Scientists Uncover How Emotions Alter Time Perception." www.psychologicalscience.org/. www.psychologicalscience.org/observer/the-fluidity-of-time.

becomes harder and loses the thrill, the time slows. If we understand that it is part of the process, the slow times are easier.

George Leonard explains the improvement cycle's effect on our emotions this way: When we start something new, we experience excitement and a rush of improvement. If we have no skill at something and try it out, it doesn't take long to improve. But these spikes don't last forever. As time goes on, eventually, we hit plateaus.[15]

These plateaus can be challenging and discouraging if we don't know they are part of the process. In the book *Talent is Overrated* by Geoff Colvin's research discovered that the better you become at something, the longer you will experience what he called flatlines. These major flatlines, or plateaus, where nothing seems to be happening or improving can be absolutely no fun and downright discouraging.

Application Corner

Exercise #1: Are You Ready to Be an Entrepreneur?

- Do you have a clear plan to weather the financial instability? (See Mistake #7)
- Are you good at time management? If not, do you have support to find a system that works for you? (See Mistake #7)
- Do you do well working long periods by yourself? Or do you have a system in place to address your social needs? (See Mistake #7)
- How well do you handle risk? Do you have guardrails to measure if you are taking too much or too little risk? (See Mistake #4)
- Do you have a clear understanding of how having your own job will meet your life goals?
- What are the reasons you want to be an entrepreneur?
- Are you good with money?

---

[15] G. Leonard. 2010. *Mastery: The Keys to Success and Long-Term Fulfillment* (Plume).

- How resilient are you? How well do you deal with setbacks, obstacles, and failures? (See Mistake #6)

  All entrepreneurs face setbacks. It is part of the game. The ability to be adaptable and resilient is a critical part of owning your own business.

- How good are you at asking for help? Delegating? And leadership? (See Mistake 12)

  No one person can have all the skills, knowledge, and resources to run a modern-day business. Asking and getting help is a must.

- How open are you to meet the market needs versus doing your own thing? (See Chapter 3)

  To create a product or service the market wants is a major component. It often requires a lot of market research.

- How good are you at tracking cash flow? Knowing how to stick to a budget is a critical part of being a successful entrepreneur.

Exercise #2: What's Your Relationship to Time?

Define your relationship with time.

Are you and time good friends and frequently go into flow together? Or do you and time work against each other?

When you plateau with a project, what can you do to keep going?

Maybe put on soothing music, drink your favorite beverage, make it a game, and so on.

Resources

Colvin, G. 2008. *Talent Is Overrated*. New York, NY: Penguin Books.
Drucker, P. 2018. *The Effective Executive*. Routledge.
Leonard, G. 2010. *Mastery: The Keys to Success and Long-Term Fulfillment*. Plume.

CHAPTER 3

Lacking Marketing/ Sales Know How

In any business, one of the chief skills is sales and marketing. There is no way to avoid it if you are running your own. If you want money coming in, you have to let people know what you offer, and you must be persuasive enough that someone says, "Yes, I want that."

According to CB Insights research, 42 percent of businesses didn't make it because there was no need for their offering.[1] This is a marketing and research issue. At the foundation, a business must know the need they meet in the market and that people want it enough to pay for it. To find out if your offer is marketable requires marketing research with potential buyers. With a rare exception, tweaks and adjustments will need to be made. A lot of entrepreneurs would like to skip making sure the market wants what they have to offer. They default to hoping their guess will work, rarely does it.

The second step of marketing is to present the offering in a language that resonates with the prospect buyer where your prospect buyer would be. Too often practitioners will write marketing copy that is reflective of insider language of what they think and feel based on their expertise and not create copy that their prospect will respond to.

The ultimate goal in all marketing copy is to have the prospect feel understood, like you understand their pain and struggle on a deep level. When you meet these criteria, they buy from you.

Some offerings are easier by nature to sell than others. The higher the risk for the buyer the more work needs to be done with the marketing.

---

[1] D. Simovic. February 25, 2022. "39 Entrepreneur Statistics You Need to Know in 2022." www.smallbizgenius.net. www.smallbizgenius.net/by-the-numbers/entrepreneur-statistics/.

For example, buying a 50-cent piece of gum is low risk. Signing up with a financial planner and letting her know all your financial information is not only risky financially but there is a lot more trust involved. Services that require more personal trust typically have a long sales cycle, and more effort is required to be in place to develop trust.

Resource

Ulwick, T. February 26, 2021. "The Core Tenets of Jobs-to-Be-Done Theory." *Medium*. JTBD + Outcome-Driven Innovation. https://jobs-to-be-done.com/the-5-tenets-of-jobs-to-be-done-theory-ba58c3a093c1.

Mistake #8: Gathering Too Much Information and Striving for an Alphabet Name

Chances are many entrepreneurs think they need to:

Weekly newsletter list
Facebook advertising
Facebook page
Instagram reels
Instagram
Pinterest
Linked-In
Twitter
Podcasts
Summits
Giveaways
Speeches
Marketing funnels
Sales funnels
Articles
Website SEO

What typically happens is the entrepreneur hears one thing and starts to figure it out, then another and goes to that, then another and on and on this goes. This person is running from place to place never really mastering and implementing anything. They become more stressed and don't achieve the results they want.

Here are some signs you are doing this:

• Lots of "to-dos" in many different areas of your business.

A deeper sign …

• You're working harder and not getting the business results you want.

Or

- The increased money you're making is not equal to the amount of additional time you are putting in.

There are two big problems here. One is making decisions based on what you "should" do. Listening to all the marketing messages about what you have to do will leave the entrepreneur confused and stressed and not be helpful. There are countless marketing strategies and business systems, and each will work differently with the kind of business and the personality doing the task. Most efforts do very little, while some things are very effective. It's a matter of finding those things that work with your natural aptitude and your ideal prospects respond to.

The second problem that can occur is when an entrepreneur slips into the pattern of learning but not implementing. Results come from implementation. I have talked with many entrepreneurs who are taking several intensive programs at once and struggle to keep up with the workload of those programs as well as their business.

In his article published in *Inc.* magazine, "Entrepreneurs May Be Susceptible to Shiny Object Syndrome," David Finkel claims that millions of entrepreneurs are affected with shiny object syndrome.[2] This means that instead of focusing on the big picture of business growth, the entrepreneur becomes sidetracked with a new idea or process that feels more exciting than what they have been doing.

This often happens because of the pain of being in the problem and the hope that a different way might relieve the discomfort. Procrastination and fear are often at play. Some estimates suggest up to 95 percent of the population procrastinates.[3]

---

[2] D. Finkel. n.d. "Entrepreneurs May Be Particularly Susceptible to Shiny Object Syndrome." www.inc.com/. www.inc.com/david-finkel/entrepreneurs-may-be-particularly-susceptible-to-shiny-object-syndrome-heres-how-to-cure-it.html (accessed May 5, 2022).

[3] C. Bailey. October 5, 2017. "5 Research-Based Strategies for Overcoming Procrastination." https://hbr.org/. https://hbr.org/2017/10/5-research-based-strategies-for-overcoming-procrastination.

It has long been believed that procrastination was a time management problem, but recently, evidence shows that suffering with mood regulation might be part of the core issue. Struggles with anxiety might cause a person to put off doing anxiety-riddled steps.

Author of *The Procrastination Equation,* Tim Pychyl, has identified triggers that might spark procrastination tendencies such as being bored, frustrated, finding the work difficult, not finding the work fun, or being unstructured.[4] Most of these triggers have an emotional undercurrent. This means all of those states of mind can be shifted.

In the *Harvard Business Review* article "Bright Shining Objects and the Future of HR," John Boudrea and Steven Rice found in their research that going after something new only provides temporary relief. The same kind of obstacle will reappear. Their recommendation is to stop being a "fad surfer"—a person that doesn't dig deep into the problem but chases the newest and greatest solution.[5] When someone is hopping from one way of doing things to another, often, they are hoping that the path to solving their problem will be easier with the newest technique.

Bourdreau and Rice recommend falling in love with the problem and going beyond the surface to achieve a big picture of the overall core issue. They also mentioned the disadvantage of being hasty to solve a solution instead of examining it from multiple angles to gain a deep understanding of what is happening.

Whether you are procrastinating by not getting to the necessary task done or diving into too much training to learn everything at once or being too quick to solve a problem, all these actions result in the same thing. They are hurting growth and might create stagnation. Learning is critical in taking your business to the next level. Through training, the entrepreneur gains the skills needed for improvement change.

But too much training and not enough implementation is a mistake, said the entrepreneurs I interviewed. This can show up when practitioners keep going for more training and certifications. The more letters they can

---

[4] Ibid.

[5] J. Boudreau and S. Rice. July 2015. "Bright, Shiny Objects and the Future of HR." https://hbr.org/. https://hbr.org/2015/07/bright-shiny-objects-and-the-future-of-hr.

pile behind their name the better. Education is always a good thing, but too many certificates and degrees can have a diminishing return. A good way to judge if you are guilty of this is if you have gone to more than three trainings in the last 90 days and haven't made it to reviewing your notes. You are guilty of information overload and/or procrastination. It's time to go on an information diet. This means not learning anything new until you have applied the most important things you have learned so far.

If the information is important but it isn't time for you to apply it to your business yet, schedule on your calendar when you think it will be a good time to revisit.

There is a balance to learning and applying. Gathering book smarts can only take you so far. It is necessary actually apply the information that you are gathering. This is the time when real learning takes place.

Sometimes, this pursuit of knowledge is a delay tactic from getting into the arena and doing business. Sometimes, it is driven by a high value for learning, but there comes a time where the entrepreneur needs to own that they know enough and spend less time learning and more time serving people with the knowledge that they already have. This means looking at the cost benefit of the training. Don't only consider the expense of the program but also the lost revenue in the time it will require away from doing revenue generating activities.

On the flip side, if you haven't gone to any training or class, you might want to attend some to empower you with the skills that would most benefit your company. It is important to keep honing and refining your skills to keep the competitive edge.

No matter the size of your business, you have limited resources. Pick only one thing to learn or skill to develop at a time. The other skills can wait and need to. Focusing on too many things at once will dilute your efforts and overwhelm you. Keep track of the other opportunities for a future date. Streamline your actions to make implementation the core application.

Sometimes, when people take a lot of classes, they question their current business model. They will hear about a different business approach that is working for someone else. They will become inspired by this model and jump into learning the new way. The problem with this is they aren't giving the current business model enough time to see if it will work. This can be a tricky one though because the entrepreneur doesn't want to waste time on techniques and models that are not working. Having a coach, consultant, or mentor who knows the industry and current trends well enough to guide you is helpful. These experts are better able to judge your efforts and advise whether to give your model more time or if another model would be a better fit.

An example of this can be found in the online industry. For many years, a 40 percent newsletter open rate was the sought-after metric. But recent changes in what can be tracked with a newsletter make that number meaningless.

Other markers are more important to watch. With this knowledge, the online business wouldn't want to throw out their newsletter efforts to do a different kind of promotion just because of low open rates. Plus, there are other tweaks that could be made such as paying more attention to subject headlines and growing your list with the right people on the newsletter. An expert would tell you what a more effective tweak would be to apply than shifting to a completely different business model.

Several entrepreneurs I interviewed talked about making the mistake of gathering too much information in software programs needed for their business. The software was high powered and could run and determine all sorts of metrics and numbers, but by the end of the day, most of those numbers were just interesting. One said it was his shiny object which he needed to put in guardrails around so he wouldn't become lost in the software numbers instead of implementing steps that would bring in more revenue.

Technology is a potentially helpful tool, but the bigger piece is knowing how it fits into the picture of your overarching goals. Having a robust software program isn't going to do any good unless it has a clear purpose in your business process. Technology is only important to a company if it could be turned into some type of competitive advantage—improving the income statement, supporting HR, making marketing, finances, turnover time better, and so forth.

A survey taken in 2018 from Udemy declared that 78 percent of the respondents admitted that their top distraction at work was using technology for personal use.[6] But according to The Hartford Report, technology saved time and most felt it made them more productive.[7]

Guardrails are a must when it comes to technology. When thinking about using the newest software in your industry, compute the amount of time it will take to learn the software versus the amount it will save in your workflow. Plus, consider carefully what structures you'll need to keep the technology as a productivity tool that minimizes distractions. For example, limiting the use of the software to doing only the tasks that will keep your project moving forward. Or have restrictions on what you will learn about the software to understand the functions that you will need in order to do your job. Have these restrictions in place until you become functional with those aspects of the program.

Application Corner

Exercise: Are You on Information Overload?

- How many conferences, trainings, and classes have you attended in the last 90 days either in person or online?
- Have you reviewed your notes and made an action plan on what things you are going to apply to your business?
- Have you applied or implemented everything you felt relevant from those events?

If you are not applying and implementing the concepts that are relevant to your business, there is a high chance that you are not implementing enough and are in information overload.

Resource

Vetter, A. August 21, 2018. "Technology Doesn't Have to Be a Distraction." www.inc.com/. www.inc.com/amy-vetter/how-to-use-technology-to-escape-distractions.html.

---

[6] "Udemy In Depth: 2018 Workplace Distraction Report." n.d. https://research.udemy.com/. https://research.udemy.com/research_report/udemy-depth-2018-workplace-distraction-report/ (accessed May 5, 2022).

[7] "The Hartford's 2016 Tech @ Work Survey." August 16, 2016. www.thehartford.com/.

Mistake #9: Lack a Grasp on Marketing and Sales

I've had my business for decades, and my biggest mistake was not studying and learning about MARKETING and SALES. When I did study it, I listened too much to the traditional funnel idea of marketing. You know the concept where prospect pays a little, then a little more, leading the prospect down the funnel to the higher ticket offer.

The problem I found with this advice is that I didn't have a business when I did it. I had a lot of little offers that gained minimal traction. Part of the problem was I didn't know what the market wanted, and I didn't know how to do the market research.

An even bigger problem was when following the advice, I didn't align what the prospect wanted with what offering aligned most with me. I learned I needed to align what I offered with my greatest skills and what the client's most wants.

When I figured out this formula, my clients started achieving huge wins, having more confidence, and having more fun. Plus, more business poured in for me.

—Linda Babulic, Executive Coach

In my interviews, mistakes in marketing ranged from investing in ineffective traditional marketing avenues to giving services away for close to free, as well as the struggle to find higher paying clients. First off, most businesses reported that the traditional marketing—ads in the newspapers, radio, billboards, TV, and magazines—didn't work. This wasn't true for every industry. This is one of those times that it is important to know your industry and what will and won't work in it.

Often the new business owner thought that the best way to become known and generate work was to buy an expensive ad in the newspaper, TV, radio, or coupon pack. They invested their money in these forms of advertisement. Almost inevitably, the results were few or no sales, and the owner was left with less money gone and still no additional clients or sales.

Be extremely careful before investing lots of funds into traditional methods of advertising. Billboards and tv marketing are structured to raise brand awareness, not sales. Big companies can afford to spend on building name recognition because they are already profitable. In addition, they know how to effectively appeal to their clients and achieve sales. Most entrepreneurs starting out do not know that yet.

Free Service Giveaways

How I became a coach was an unusual one. I was an author first. Back in the old days, authors were often asked to speak at live events. After the speeches, people would approach me, asking if I would work with them.

I always answered, "But I am not a therapist."

And they would say they didn't care.

Finally, I decided to try it out. It turned out that it was something I had been doing my whole life.

Two years into playing around with coaching, I decided to become serious about it and become certified. Imagine my surprise when I was in the middle of coaching class and the instructor gave directions about coaching for free or charging very little so the newbie coach could get their feet wet.

The problem with pro-bono work is the person receiving the help often doesn't value it as much as they would if they were paying for it. Paying means investing in themselves and their future. That is needed for the client to show up at their best. They need to say that they are worth it and want the promise of the service they are paying for. That is a different energy than someone getting it for free.

Another reason you need to be careful of doing free work is the time involved takes away from making a living. Sometimes, entrepreneurs will offer to do free work as a way of avoiding sales conversations or because of lack of confidence in the quality of their work. Others do it to gain experience. But, having the money conversation is part of the owner's experience that is critical to their business future.

Although, there are situations when doing something for free is good to do. For example, an entrepreneur is asked to give speeches. If the speaking opportunity is legitimate exposure to their right audience then that is a valid way of growing one's business. For the entrepreneur to make it worth their time, they need to know the worth and value of the speaking engagement and be strategic on how they set up the speech.

If appropriate, provide a free gift in exchange for the e-mail address of the audience members, a common strategy.

Of course, there is also decreasing fees or doing service for free as a way of giving back. Giving back and supporting those in need is important, but if it becomes the center of your business, it will be hard to stay in business. Implementing a sliding scale and other ways to support those who can't afford the full service can be part of your business model.

A mentor once counselled me a good rule of thumb is to offer 20 percent of clients the sliding scale. That way the business will not be too impacted, and the entrepreneur can still offer their service to those who would not otherwise be able to receive the help.

Another strategy that many entrepreneurs do is providing free or low-cost offerings. Some multimillionaire entrepreneurs provide hundreds of videos on YouTube as a way to provide help to everyone. This generous giving builds their name and the awareness of their work. Other entrepreneurs encapsulate their knowledge in books, newsletters, and free or low-cost lead magnets.

Some entrepreneurs become sucked up in the service trap that might get them known in the community but not for their business. These entrepreneurs volunteer for so many associations and groups that they rarely have time to work in their own business. This might be more harmful than helpful to them.

Competing Against the Big Guys

Another big concern with marketing and sales is the competition. Competing against the big corporation has never been easier. I'm not saying it is easy, but with many of the available tools, the small guys have a good chance. We now have at our fingertips the ability to reach potential customers across the world at no or low price through social media, podcasts, Clubhouse, e-mail services, and other evolving platforms. Yes, the big companies do pull their weight to squeeze out the little guy with dominating Facebook advertising and Amazon product preferences, but the little guys still have a chance. They can and do find ways to be successful in the competitive marketplace. Often, they are able to shake up the traditional way of doing things, case in point Airbnb and Uber.

Uber competed with taxi cab companies with a strategy that a taxi cab company couldn't do without losing or hurting their business. Cab companies had to own expensive medallions to operate, hire employees, and buy their own vehicles. But since Uber was an upstart, they hired independent contractors, owned no vehicles, and leveraged an app to dramatically improve the customer experience. Riders benefited because it was less expensive, more convenient, and a better experience.

Airbnb competed in a similar fashion. Both companies carved out a spot in the marketplace because their idea was new and their business model was hard to go against.

The ease of building online campaigns revolutionized marketing in the past 5 to 10 years. You don't have to be tech savvy or learn much html in order to build online systems and automation.

Power of the Nimble

Another amazing advantage a small business has over the large companies is their ability to be nimble and more responsive. When the crash of 2008 happened, I was able to change my business that day. Many smaller companies did similar things with the COVID-19 shutdown. Big companies generally can't shift that quickly. They have more systems and politics to maneuver through. When you are dealing with more people and more systems, it is harder to adjust as fast to the market changes and to implement feedback. In fact, small companies have a greater ability to solicit customer's feedback in deeper and more meaningful ways.

Power of the Personal

Customers on the whole like to work with people who understand them, their ethics, their lives, and their businesses. It presents more of a challenge for the bigger corporations to give their customers this feeling.

Recently, my financial planner and his team were separating from their firm. As a customer, I was presented with the choice to stay with the institution or go with the financial planner to a different company. For those of you who have experienced this, you know as the customer, when a business separation happens, both sides race to secure as many clients as possible.

In my situation, I suddenly received an onslaught of phone calls from both sides, each trying to convince me to go one direction or the other. Ultimately after weighing out the pros and cons of both sides, my decision boiled down to the relationship I had with the secretary.

She had sent me flowers when my husband was in the ICU. She had always taken her time to find out how I and my children were doing. Those small touches over the years build the sense of trust that she had my back. That trust ultimately mattered above and beyond the other considerations

As a side note, before I could make the move, the institution I was originally at assigned me to some random person who made no effort in finding out about me or how to support my family. On the one phone call I had with him, he was dismissive and wanting to go to the next call. I knew that my account wasn't large enough for him to care.

The secretary's personal touch created a deep loyalty so I moved with her group. The cold administrative approach of the other group created resentment and relief I was no longer with that company.

Short-Term Panic Drives Customers Away

Recently, a big coaching outfit contacted me. I sat through their entire scripted sales call, and then at the end, they pitched me a high-ticket offer that would go for a year. The product wasn't in alignment with my next quarter goals, but I could see it being helpful in the future. I declined for now.

Instead of responding in a professional way, saying he understood and asking if he could touch base again in four months, the salesperson was short and dismissive. It felt like he was pouting that I had said no. That took away any consideration of working with that organization in the future.

I knew that salesperson wasn't reflective of the whole organization, but my thinking was if a person isn't respectful the first time a prospect says "not now" to a high-ticket offer, then that salesperson lacks the maturity I want for support.

Another outfit was talking to me about their program. I was very interested in it, but I needed time to look over the program's offerings.

They asked me if I would sign up then and there. I said no. I had a family member in my house just come down with COVID. We were in the waiting period to see if the whole family would become sick or if we had it contained. We had several people in the house that were high risk. I wasn't going to commit to a high-ticket offer that I might not have time for until I had a better idea of what I was dealing with in my personal life.

The salesperson said they would send an e-mail with the detail information about their program and would call the next week to check-in, when I had a better idea of what I was dealing with.

At the end of the call, he asked the traditional sales question, "How committed are you to this?"

I was a 7.

What would make it a 10?

I needed to see if this was the right direction for my business and if it was the right time.

That salesperson never sent me the information about the program and never called.

Both of these salespeople assumed that my no was a permanent no. But was that true? Let's look at the statistics on sales after follow-ups. Sixty percent of customers say no four times before buying, and 70 percent of salespeople stop after one sales call.[8] The math is mixed up. So the salesperson was trying to sell me a high-ticket offer with one sales call. He had more than a 60 percent chance of me saying no, actually greater since I didn't know much about this company. This was my first real exposure to it. If he was on his game, he at least would have sent me the brochure so I would have a visual reference of the services he offered. It might be more information that I was asking for, but it also would have given one more touch point that the company was legitimate. Instead, the salesperson put a bad taste in my mouth for the company's services. His lack of understanding of where I was in the sales process and how my personal life was impacting my decision caused the company to miss out on my future business.

---

[8] A. Frost. May 6, 2022, "60 Key Sales Statistics That'll Help You Sell Smarter in 2021," *HubSpot Blog* (HubSpot). https://blog.hubspot.com/sales/salesstatistics#:~:text=Sales%20Follow%2DUp%20Statistics&text=60%25%20of%20customers%20say%20no,after%20one%20follow%2Dup%20call.

Which is too bad, because I found value in the company's services, and I could have easily signed up if I was treated with more consideration. Both programs had the ability to solve a significant problem I was having, but their lack of patience and follow-through made me distrust them enough to look for a different solution.

We have all seen many prospects decline an offer, and then a year goes by, and the service provider checks in with the prospect who buys this time. Some of us have been those people. Sometimes, it is because nothing has improved in their world with the problem or the problem became worse. Or the person's life is in a better place to focus on that particular area. Or …. Or … Or.

Proper follow-up is critical to maintaining consistent sales. One of the big reasons entrepreneurs stop approaching someone is they don't want to be "that guy." We have all experienced them.

You say no, and they keep hounding you. I had a peer do that to me recently. He was hosting a weekly event that I was attending partly to show support and partly because I like being in the community of like-minded individuals.

The peer did a long launch. I attended all his events and helped spread the word about his product to show him support. He sent me an e-mail about his program which was similar to the work I do. He wanted me to sign up. I didn't respond. He e-mailed me over five more times. I ignored the messages, thinking he was a bit determined.

He sent me a Loom video and asked if we could meet. We met. He wanted to know why I didn't sign up. I went into detail that we were peers, and I didn't need what he had to offer but appreciated his work and in fact referred out his material.

Did he stop there? No. I received at least five more e-mails and videos to get me to sign up for something I had no interest in.

That guy.

From my experience with entrepreneurs, most don't want to become that person.

So how do you find the balance of following up and giving the support that the prospect needs to eventually sign up with your program without being that guy?

The biggest determining factor is your follow-up approach. If you show up with an attitude of service, you will avoid being that annoying person. That can look like sending an e-mail with additional tips that you think might help the prospect. Or touching base with a genuine desire to see where the person is at and looking for ways to help them even if it is not what you offer.

Part of this approach is knowing if the prospect needs what you are offering. If they are doing a similar thing in the workplace, they aren't a prospect. Looking for ways to partner might be a good option.

If they are no longer in the field that you serve, they are no longer a prospect, but that doesn't mean that they don't know someone who might benefit from what you have. Bottom line, treat each prospect as a human being and put the relationship above the sale. When you only show up because you think you can get something out of them, that lacks professionalism and burns bridges.

Reality of a Sales Force

The number one thing the owner looks for is finding a salesperson to be on their team, but finding the right salesperson is no easy task. When I worked in a successful start-up that was beginning to take off, the biggest challenge was finding people who had proper sales training. The owner even hired a recruiting agency but that didn't help.

According to U.S. Small Business Administration, it will cost the owner between 1.25 to 1.4 times the salesperson's salary to bring someone onboard.[9] Despite the challenge of finding people who are properly trained in sales and the cost of bringing them onboard, there is also the added pressure of training them to be effective with your product or service.

Then there is the fact that only 3 percent of consumers trust sales reps.[10] And the challenge of selling is no easy task.[11] Most often, the salesperson will not be as effective as the owner. It is the owner who cares the most and understands the value of the product or service the most deeply.

[9] B. Weltman. August 22, 2019. "How Much Does an Employee Cost You?" www.sba.gov/. https://www.sba.gov/blog/how-much-does-employee-cost-you.

[10] "149 Eye-Opening Sales Stats to Consider in 2022." December 6, 2021. https://spotio.com/. https://spotio.com/blog/sales-statistics/.

[11] S. Sampat. n.d. "20 Statistics You Need to Know Before Hiring Your First Salesperson." https://smith.ai. https://smith.ai/blog/20-statistics-you-need-to-know-before-hiring-your-first-salesperson (accessed May 5, 2022).

The owner no matter where they are with their business needs to stay involved in the sales process. This will keep them in touch with the market and empower them in the decisions they are making in leading their company. Those owners who are too distant from the reality of their customers will not make the best decisions.

Application Corner

Exercise #1: Marketing Tool Audit

List your best marketing tool.
Does it fit your personality?
Are you gaining traction from using it?
What can you do to make it more effective?

Exercise #2: Volunteer Audit

If you have a volunteer bug, it is important to do an audit on your time and see how that is translating to the bottom line.
Also look at the why you are volunteering.

Is it out of obligation instead or passion?
Is it because you have a hard time saying no?
Are you out of alignment with any of the associations?
Are you being treated with respect and valued?
Does the association have the scope of impact you are wanting to make?

If volunteerism is having too much of a negative influence on your business, consider picking your favorite association, serve there, and limit your service to the others.

Exercise #3: A Competitor Analysis

What advantages do you have over your competitor?
What small, personalized touches can you put into your current day-to-day operations that would create value for your current customers?

What world events are impacting business?

How can you respond to the current climate in a way that shows deep understanding of your clients and prospects' challenges?

Resources

"Billboards for Small Businesses: 7 Reasons to Think Twice." n.d. www.verizon.com/. www.verizon.com/business/small-business-essentials/resources/billboards -small-businesses-7-reasons-think-twice-021956544/ (accessed May 5, 2022).

Hickey, J. n.d. "Social Media Marketing Is Costly and Far Less Effective Than It Once Was. Here's What to Do Instead." www.inc.com/. www.inc.com/ jordan-hickey/social-media-marketing-alternatives-loyal-customers.html (accessed May 5, 2022).

Mistake #10: Make It About You, Not Them

Some people make a mistake thinking that others actually care about them and why they are in business. Unless it is a family member, your best friend, current client, and maybe your spouse or partner, most people are worried about their own problems. Seriously, people are not going to think, "whose product or service can I buy today? Who would I like to give money to?" There is too much competition out there for consumers' time, energy, and money.

Sounds obvious, but go to five websites and check them out. Does the website talk all about the person promoting the product? I don't want to pick on coaches, but I'm going to give in to temptation because they are a perfect example. Go to five life coach websites, and you will more likely than not find a website with a home page full of a big smiling face. If done well, the site will be full of calming colors and nice graphics. The words will more than likely be about who they are and why they are in business. That is great, but no one cares unless it's just for the entertainment value or has some other appeal to them.

Coaches or other business owners who use this approach are making the mistake of thinking that a ton of information about them will matter to the potential client or customer. The prospect cares about whether you can solve their problem or supply something they need. So, what does a website look like that is customer-focused?

A home page is customer-focused when the language above the fold shows the entrepreneur's solution to the prospect's pain. That is it. It has been done in many different ways, but from the moment a prospect lands on your web page, the ideal prospect needs to feel that you know them. You know their pain, and you have the answer for them.

More updated websites often stand out from the websites that are stuck in the style that has become outdated. Websites that go deeper into the customer's pain always stand out from the websites that focus too much on the person offering the service unless that person is extremely famous. Too much focus on the owner is a big tale that particular business doesn't understand their prospect well enough. If they did understand their prospect, the website wouldn't focus on the business owner but on their niche and the prospect's wants and desires.

It sounds simple. It isn't. To truly understand your ideal prospect's greatest need, you need to know your niche. The biggest mistake I see with entrepreneurs is they have a vague idea of who their ideal client is or claiming that they help everyone. Narrowing down your niche is intensive work. One of the goals is to narrow down enough that others understand who you serve and the problem you solve.

Here are a few guidelines to see if you are specific enough:

1. When mentioning who you serve, do people say, "Oh, I know someone that needs that." Or "You know who you should really talk to?" A great way to test if others get who your ideal clients is mentioning who you are looking for at a network meeting and see how it lands.
2. Do you know where you would find your niche both online and in person? If you were going to throw a big party for your ideal prospects, where would you go to make the invitation? What would be the best way to let them know about your party? What kind of party would produce the biggest turnout? Why would they want to come?
3. Do you know what they would find most appealing about your product or service?
4. What would attract their attention even on a hard and stressful day?
5. Do they prefer positive images or negative ones? Why?

This intense work is critical to the success of your marketing and sales efforts.

I interviewed several companies that help entrepreneurs go online. They stated that their clientele's greatest issue preventing them from being successful online was not being properly niched and not knowing who they serve.

Knowing your niche, their needs, their wants, and the language they use to describe their struggles is foundational for an online business.[12]

---

[12] J. Hickey. n.d. "Social Media Marketing Is Costly and Far Less Effective Than It Once Was. Here's What to Do Instead." https://www.inc.com/. www.inc .com/jordan-hickey/social-media-marketing-alternatives-loyal-customers.html (accessed May 5, 2022).

This information is important to have drilled down before creating website copy, social media posts, brochures, and producing newsletters.

Standing Out in a Crowded Market

In one of my interviews, I asked a salesperson how he achieved a competitive edge over others in his profession? He smiled and said, "I am a different color than all the other salespeople here. When I come around, the doctors remember me."

Go with what you have. What is different about you that sticks out from the crowd? Perhaps, signature clothing, hair, accessory, or ability can be useful. There was one person in the speaking world who made it big just because he wore a name tag announcing his name everywhere he went.

Sometimes, it is not looks that helps you stand out. It could be the way you pitch your service that achieves the heart of the issue for the business, or it could be your friendly nature that just makes everyone feel welcome and seen.

Each of us is unique and has something to offer. Knowing what that is and bringing it out will set you apart in the marketplace. One of the reasons so many of us struggle with it is we have been with ourselves so long we aren't conscious of how we stand out or even worse we think everyone is like us or has our skill. But the good news is other people know what your uniqueness is and how you standout so ask them.

Not everyone is going to resonate with your uniqueness, and by embracing it, some entrepreneurs are afraid that it will limit their market. As the old saying goes "niche to get rich." You will attract more of the right people by being seen and allowing the right people to find you.

When I was first starting my coaching practice, I had no idea how to be visible. I was just a stay-at-home mother turned coach. To make matters worse, at the time not many people even knew what coaching was. I was often asked what sport I was coaching.

Nowadays, the market is flooded with coaches, so the challenge is different. Back then, I worked with a marketing specialist, who said my uniqueness was the number of children I had, the radio show I was on, and the number of books I had published.

The radio show and the number of books published I had no issue using and could see would set me apart, but using the fact that I was a mother of seven (at the time now it's eight) hurt my stomach. I knew that being a mother wasn't always welcome in the marketplace, and I have had more than one radio show host ask me if I knew about birth control. None of these things I welcomed.

But over the years, I have also received additional feedback. Yes, I work with a high percentage of mothers. Many of them have told me they worked with me because they knew I knew what it was like running a business and raising children.

When interviewing for a contract job, I was also told that being a mother with six children so far graduated from college showed that I knew how to be organized and how to work and motivate different personalities to pursue education. I had developed skills balancing work/life issues and had excellent time management skills.

Most of you will not be a parent of eight children, but you have something unique that you might feel as uncomfortable putting out there. I was afraid of the judgment and the disapproval. I did receive a lot of that, but by me owning how I stood out in the marketplace; the clients who were a perfect fit were able to find me because I didn't hide how I was different. I spotlighted who I was, and they could decide faster if that worked for them or not.

My story also told the prospects about my value system: six of my children so far have achieved a college degree, which I hope reveals how important education is to me. Plus, I know how to hold people accountable since clearly all my children know how to meet deadlines that is required to be successful in school. It might also suggest I know how to do the mother eyebrow raise and call people on their excuses.

When the subject of how many children I have comes up in the media, I almost immediately state that I don't recommend it or offer to sell a couple of my young adults. No one has ever taken me up on the offer. But with those comments, I am communicating part of my personality, and that I most likely don't fit into mold that someone would naturally put the mother of eight in.

How you put together letting others know how you are unique in the marketplace will be highlighted in the story you tell. The story communicates your values, your commitments, and your identity and is a critical part of setting you apart and who you will attract.

Appreciation Cards on Odd Holidays

Another way to stand out in an overcrowded market is through handwritten cards. Sending your customers a card on Christmas has become almost expected but on Halloween? That will pop. Just like a personalized handwritten note stands out from a generic card with just a signature or signatures.

Most ofter, if you want to acknowledge a customer's birthday and send them a 10 percent coupon, that will not land well with the customer unless they were already thinking of buying that service anyway. Giving a coupon feels like a sales promotion. Giving a free session or gift feels like a birthday celebration.

Focus on Values Your Customers Have

According to the survey done by ZypMedia, consumers would prefer to buy something local rather than national.[13] They found that the consumers wanted to support the local economy (54 percent) and local community (84 percent). This survey was conducted during the COVID-19 pandemic, so it remains to be seen if this trend will continue, but it most likely will. People tend to want to help those in their community. They generally sense that the local people understand their circumstances, values, and culture better.

---

[13] ZypMedia. May 28, 2020, "Consumers Want to Support Their Local Economy by Supporting Local Businesses, According to a Survey by ZypMedia." www.prnewswire.com/news-releases/consumers-want-to-support-their-local-economy-by-supporting-local-businesses-according-to-a-survey-by-zypmedia-301066610.html.

Application Corner

Exercise #1: Website Check-In: Is It About Them?

Have someone in your target market review your website, marketing material, and other promotional strategies.

Have them rate on a 1 to 5 scale:

- How closely does the material speak to their pain?
- Do they know and understand who would be an ideal fit for this service or product?
- How modern do they find the style, font, and graphics?
- Is expertise established?
- How compelled are they to find out more?

Exercise #2: Standing Out in a Crowded Marketplace

Write down how you stand out and attract business.

Consider what you could do or be or give to customers that would be memorable to them.

Example: Have a bigger size business card. Dye your hair purple. Embrace humor. Use bold unusual colors in your copy. Add something unexpected in your presentations or marketing material. Celebrate your uniqueness. Dress better than your competition.

Resource

"Niche Marketing—Entrepreneur Small Business Encyclopedia." n.d. www .entrepreneur.com/ (accessed May 5, 2022).

CHAPTER 4

Stepping Into the Quicksand of Poor Relationship Skills

At the root of all business are relationships. A recent survey found that relationships outdo any other consideration in business. Eighty-six percent of those surveyed said they are willing to pay more for a better customer experience.[1] Improved customer relations increases cross-selling and upselling, customer retention, and customer satisfaction. In the entrepreneur world, better relationships also increase better marketing, sales, and team development.

Relationships are complex. Let's look at the common mistakes entrepreneurs make in this realm.

Mistake #11: Didn't Understand How People Work

Often in the business world, return on investment (ROI) has a lot of buzz, but Ted Rubin, a popular social media strategist, claims RonR (return on relationships) is more important. He defines RonR as "the value that is accrued by a person or brand due to nurturing a relationship."[2]

Research reveals that entrepreneurs who put relationships in the forefront are rewarded with a huge boost in their business. The finding also discovered that entrepreneurs who use the skills of relationship marketing do better. People like doing business with people they know, like, and trust. The findings are not surprising. Relationships play a crucial role.[3]

[1] T. Kulbyte. June 24, 2021. "Key Customer Experience Statistics to Know." www.superoffice.com/. www.superoffice.com/blog/customer-experience-statistics/.

[2] T. Rubin. n.d. 'Return on Relationship," *Ted Rubin*. www.ror.online/.

[3] J. Day, A.A. Dean, and P.L. Reynolds. July 24, 2002. "Relationship Marketing: Its Key Role in Entrepreneurship," *Long Range Planning* (Pergamon). www .sciencedirect.com/science/article/abs/pii/S0024630198800198.

Seventy-four percent of the small business owners and entrepreneurs I interviewed brought up the absolute importance of relationships. This is the number one thing that determined whether their business was successful or not. There is no magic advertising or technique that is more powerful than relationships. It applies to all areas from the way you treat your employees to your support team, to your clients, and the people that you team up with. Look at your relationships, and you will see the future of your business.

Burning Bridges

Some business owners and entrepreneurs I interviewed didn't realize the impact it would have on their business to burn bridges or, in other words, break off a relationship with someone in a way that would not be able to be restored easily. They reflected that the impact was worse and lasted longer than they could have ever thought.

When bridges get burned, it is amazing how it can come back and bite. One person mentioned how awful the strained relationship became. She and the person she had the altercation with both worked with the same clientele on a regular basis. They were unable to keep a professional air when their paths crossed. It negatively reflected on both of them, and their clients started looking for other alternatives.

Another person gave public speeches defaming a well-known person in the industry. This fueled the feud and left a bad taste in the audience mouth and reflected badly on the person gossiping. People stopped doing business with the person who was bad-mouthing out of fear that they would be next.

One of my interviewees stated that although he was tempted to burn bridges, he didn't and was surprised to receive a prized referral from the person he had been tempted to bad-mouth. Others reported later doing highly lucrative collaborations with the person they had wanted to bad-mouth.

But is it right to always play nice and maintain relationships? The sad answer is no. According to Martha Stout, the author of the bestselling book *The Sociopath Next Door*, one out of twenty-six people are sociopaths. These are people who lack conscious and often take pure joy in destroying another person's life. It can be over simple petty things like they think you are prettier than them or receiving the attention that they think merits them, not you.

Stout's advises when running into them is to get out of their lives as much as possible.[4] Jumping out of this type of relationship might require burning bridges. Another time that might require burning bridges is when you are working in a company or with a partnership with someone who doesn't have the same morals or ethics as you do and it is causing you stress. Though it might be painful to sever the relationship, removing yourself from an ethical issue as soon as possible and with professionalism is advisable.

Didn't Understand People

The extremely successful businesspeople I interviewed often mentioned how understanding people was what helped them get to where they are. Knowing how people work and how to interact with different personalities is a critical skill.

I have often found, working with small business owners, that there is a reason why they are the president of their own company. They are innately good at what they do. They understand their company the best, and they care the most. What sometimes happens with these high-functioning individuals is that they don't grasp that the gifts they bring to the business are unusual. If they don't understand that their level of performance is higher than what others are capable of doing, they can become frustrated with their employees that don't perform the way they expected. Some take this as a personal afront when really it is not understanding that people work differently from each other.

The owners are the owner for a reason. If their employees had the same skill set, they wouldn't be working for the owner. They would be an owner themselves. It is a unique balance to set the right expectations with employees and understand that people are built with different abilities and skill sets. *US Veterans Magazine* highlighted 15 differences between owners and employees. Entrepreneurs have a higher tolerance for risk;

---

[4] M. Stout. 2005. *The Sociopath Next Door* (Harmony).

they own the results of their work. Employees have lower tolerance of risk and are more task-focused. Also, the need for the owner to always be selling contrasts with employees who work to complete tasks.[5]

Awareness of the Impact on Your Team

Another part of unifying the team is making sure that as a leader you can see or understand each member's perception about the objective. I had a client whose boss came to the team huddle declaring that he needed to make another $100,000 in the next quarter so he could go on more exotic trips. Needless to say, that wasn't inspiring to the rest of the team and gave them plenty to talk about that wasn't in favor of his income increasing and their workload doubling.

Once a dean at one of the lowest-paying community colleges in the United States asked for the teachers to give up 20 percent of their income to go to the less fortunate. He did not think about the fact that he was earning a high six-figure income, while the teachers were struggling to pay bus fair and rent.

One upstart went on social media raging about how he had a standard that his employees must meet, and he would not lower his bar. Part of that high standard was for the employees to have only Christmas Day off and to continue to work the insane hours continuously with no bonuses. After he went on his social media rant, many of his employees resigned.

Leaders sometimes become so caught up in the ROI; they forget about understanding the RonR of the lives of their employees and how they will view the initiative.

Meaningful Interactions With Your Clients or Customers

Part of understanding people is understanding your clients or customers. According to the Forrester report, "Out of The Crisis, A New Order Takes Hold" concluded that companies need to be focusing on "how

---

[5] "15 Differences Between Employees and Entrepreneurs." March 15, 2019. https://usveteransmagazine.com/. https://usveteransmagazine.com/2019/03/15-differences-employees-entrepreneurs.

customer-obsessed resilient, creative, and adaptive you are jumping to the next growth curve in your industry."[6]

The most significant message of this entire report is the emphasis for businesses to make meaningful interactions with their clients. The pace of doing business has accelerated, making it more stressful for many. It is helpful to be sensitive to that fact when interacting with others. Coming from a place of compassion best serves our clients. This will make it as easy as possible for your clients to have their needs met through your services or products.

To ensure that you are giving the ease to your clients, look at your service, your products, your deliverables, and your e-mails. Analyze the best way to serve your clients in their current circumstances and then focus on attracting new clients.

Cultivating Your Inner Circle

When thinking about relationships, rarely do we look at our connections with those surrounding us and if that is supportive for us. Those we allow into our sphere of influence can have a huge impact, not only on our decisions but also subtle things like our energy and productivity levels.

An effective way to know how you are doing in this area is to take a few minutes and jot down the five people who you spend the most time with. Look at the list. Are these people a positive or a negative? If they are a positive, great.

A person who is a positive in your life is someone who you can go to when you are down and they will have your back. When you have a win, they are happy for you. They genuinely want the best for you.

A negative person is someone who looks at the worse side of life and criticizes and complains. This is a person who will not be looking out for your best interest, and you are not sure if you can trust them. Be sure to note that there is a difference between someone who is a bit of a

---

[6] "Accelerating Out of the Crises." November 17, 2021 www.biia.com/, (Forrester), p. 2. www.biia.com/wp-content/uploads/2020/11/Forrester_Predictions_2021 .pdf.

downer and has your back and someone who is harmful, puts you down, self-absorbed, selfish, gives you bad advice on purpose, and spreads hurtful rumors. If the people in your life have qualities of both positive and negative qualities, rate them on which side do they lean toward.

An important thing to think about as you consider all this is if they do have some negativity and you value what they bring to your life. Are you willing to do the work to counteract any negative impact?

To create a powerful supportive environment, make sure you are around at least one individual who is one or two steps ahead of what you want to accomplish. This will not only help you to know what steps to take but also will serve as proof that your aspirations are possible.

It is helpful to be in a community where others are in the same or similar situation that you are in. This can be incredibly encouraging to be surrounded by other people who understand the goods, wins, and the struggles. It is important to be around people who are actually doing things, taking risks, and living life and not have the influence of those who have settled.

Thinking about all this: being encouraged, being around people who are playing a big game, being around people who are moving forward, look again at your list of five people you spend the most time with. Do you want to make some changes? If the people on your list don't completely fit it, it becomes important to create space for those who will.

If you feel that your support system could use some boosting, there are several things that you could do to improve your situation. You could join a local business group. You could find a coach or mentor. You could join a program that is specifically designed to help you receive the support you need to be there for you as you move forward. In this type of program, you will be going through the material at the same time as your peers.

The advantage of getting into a group that is designed to support you in taking action is that you will not only be with others in a similar situation but you will soon see how you are unique on what you offer and be able to form powerful alliances and deep friendships that could propel your business dramatically forward.

Application Corner

Exercise #1: Motivating Team Through Understanding Their Needs and Wants

How do you motivate the people on your team?
How effective is it?
What is it that your team wishes you understood about them?
What do you need to learn to be an even more effective leader?

Exercise #2: Unifying Your Team

A common purpose can inspire everyone on a team. A mission or goal or aspiration will keep the team moving forward when times are challenging. When things become muddled, the common purpose can pull the team back together.

What is your common purpose?

Does it inspire everyone on your team? If not, you might not have a cultural fit or more work needs to be done on refining the common purpose.

Resource

Council, Forbes Human Resources. March 5, 2018. "Council Post: 10 Simple Ways to Get to Know Your Employees Better." *Forbes*. Forbes Magazine. www.forbes.com/sites/forbeshumanresourcescouncil/2018/03/05/10-simple-ways-to-get-to-know-your-employees-better/?sh=5877e54e4b97.

Mistake #12: Hiring Errors

The business owners interviewed who had a team often talked about the rough ride of hiring the right candidate. They found that skills could be taught by a good mentor or teacher, but a great attitude on life could not. Most of the battle of having a great team is who you hire and how they fit into the company culture. That means looking at things beyond the surface and being aware of your own bias and how it might play out in your hiring practice.

I worked with an up-and-coming entrepreneur who built a successful software company. When the company launched, he and his friend worked around the clock. Their business grew, and the demand increased to the point they needed to hire people. When we were talking about his growing pains, he commented that hiring married women brought too many problems, especially when the job required her to work long hours with a male.

The women on his team had different lifestyle, values, ways of communicating, and worries. This young entrepreneur found all of this problematic. He lacked the skills to cope with the friction. He believed that dealing with issues that rose up from that situation was a distraction and taking him away from being productive. Since our conversation about the value of having people with a different perceptive and insight on the team, he has found women to be a major asset in the company. It has more than paid off for him to challenge his hiring biases and grow in his leadership abilities.

As entrepreneurs, it is common to bump up against our personal edge. Shifting from being a solo-entrepreneur to managing a team requires growth. Value can come from having people different from ourselves on our staff. The wealth of information, insight, and fresh perspective far outweighs the pains that come with learning how to create a supportive work environment.[7]

In the following quote, Bruce Peck, CEO of Approachable Geek, highlights his hiring mistakes and how he fixed them. You will notice that his mistake at taking whoever they can find is a common one for business owners who are starting out and desperate for help.

---

[7] G. Hinde. December 10, 2020. "4 Hiring Bias Study Statistics That May Shock You—IQ Partners." www.iqpartners.com.

The biggest hiring mistakes I have made thus far all have a few things in common: not having a large sample size of candidates and not testing them rigorously against clear criteria that correlate with job performance.

The first hires we made we didn't have a clearly defined process or strategy to ensure we were hiring a great fit. We would hire the first person that sounded like they could do the job. We followed this until we had about 6 people in the company, and ended up firing all of them, going back to me and my co-founder. The ironic thing is that we were way more productive with 2 rather than 6.

Now we make sure that for every hire we look at 100 applications, grade them against objective criteria, ask them questions that relate to those criteria, have them do a project that reflects what they would do on a daily basis and then have a final interview with our company checking for culture fit.

We have our system streamlined now so we can go through a hiring process in two weeks and hire great candidates. Plus, the people interviewing love it because they can get feedback quickly and clearly.
—Bruce Peck, CEO of Approachable Geek

It took Peck time to develop a system that helped him truly find the best candidate both in skill level and culture fit, but the time he took to implement paid off well in the long run.

How to Bridge the Hiring Gap

One of the big struggles of entrepreneurs as they grow is they often will fall into the gap. The gap is when the work that is needed to be done is more than one person or their small team can handle, but the income coming in is not enough to generate paying for the new hire. This is a painful chokehold.

A solution that many entrepreneurs go with at this point is hire contract work. This provides relief because most of the time the pay structure is centered around paying the contractor only when they do work and that happens only when work is coming in. But the entrepreneur can become too dependent on contractors and a contractor's availability is not guaranteed. There will come a point where it would be more prudent to let go of the contractors and hire one in-house employee whose priority would be to work for your company. In the long run, this can be a more affordable and sustainable option.

How to Find the Money to Pay Your New Hires

1. **Focus on income-generating activities.** By hiring someone else, you just bought yourself more time to grow the company and put in systems for scaling. If you hired a salesperson, you just multiplied your efforts.
2. **Raise your prices.** You are giving more support and more value. This is a great way to generate fast cash with urgency. For example: "Want to get in now before the price increases?" "Want to be trained with me involved? Need to sign up now." Or, "Prices are going up next quarter to pay for my new hire."
3. **Ask for referrals from people who have sent you business or have worked with you.** "Who are three people you know who might need this right now?"
4. **Upsell current clients.** What are the next-level problems clients are having? With more support on your team, your time will be freed up to create higher-level signature programs and products.
5. **Grants and loans.** Look into the grants available. Business owners are often surprised at how many they can qualify for. Another option is securing a loan. Leverage credit can be used to go faster. If you go this route, calculate the investment, and know exactly how you are going to the get the money back. Securing a loan can compress time. There are companies that offer loans with low interest rates.

Streamline the Onboarding Process With New Hires

One of the reasons entrepreneurs are resistant to hiring is all the time and effort it takes to train a new employee. The owner needs to take time away from their work or pay an employee to do the training. At the beginning of the process, it runs the business at a loss.

Some companies deal with this by having no onboarding process whatsoever, but that practice leaves the new hire feeling lost and resentful.

The new hires also won't know the company's process later on. This will hurt the company to not take time to ensure the employee is successful.

One way to offset and lessen the loss is to become strategic on how you do onboarding. Modern-day technology has made it easier. One simple tactic that the employer can implement long before they hire someone is to record themselves doing a task that is often duplicated.

Creating a library of videos showing how to do various tasks makes it so that the new hire can basically train themselves on many critical aspects of the business. They have the reference of the video to revisit giving them more independence figuring out their tasks.

If onboarding through a video process appeals to you, once you have done the videos on the major tasks, make sure that you do these various videos:

- A welcome video;
- Explain the company's big goal and vision;
- Highlight the company's culture;
- Outline the role the person is hired for, why that role is needed, and the expectations and metrics they will be evaluated by;
- Detail company's clients, the clients' biggest concerns, frequently asked questions.

To appeal to various learners, it would be helpful to also make handouts covering the most important points you want your new hiree to understand and have an easy reference too.

By creating a video library, it might feel time-consuming, but if you integrate the videos into your daily work, it will not be as daunting, and in the long run, you will save yourself hours of training time.

Application Corner

Exercise: Clarity on Personality Type for Position

What personality type would be best for the position that you are hiring?
What personality traits do you don't have that be a great contribution to the team?
What personality type do you best work with?
How important is it for them to be teachable?

Mistake #13: Didn't Look to Others for Help

A super common mistake that entrepreneurs make is not accepting support in their ventures. They looked at building their business as a lone ranger activity when in fact in order to build a successful business, the help of others is required, and the ability to be able to receive help is mandatory.

Sometimes, people have a hard time letting go of doing what they have always done. Plus, they don't trust others will do it right. Well, the truth is most likely a lot of the support staff *won't* do it as well as them and that just might be ok if it is "good enough" and frees the leader to do more important activities.

But, oftentimes, the new person might do it better than the owner. The new person brings different skills, knowledge, and experience to the task and also gives the project a fresh glance.

Such fierce independence was fundamental to those entrepreneurs to get them where they are at. But to get where they want to go requires more hands, and more input from others and moved into a launch and scale mindset.

The Antidote to Being Too Rogue

If you see yourself in the above scenario of always wanting to go at it alone, the antidote is to practice receiving and giving support. This is often a new set of skills for the rugged independent type and will require conscious focus.

In one of my professional associations, there was a businessman that dominated his industry and one of the few who was experiencing big success during the recession. He told me that when he first joined the association, he joined for the wrong reasons. He joined strictly for what was in it for him and what he could get out of it.

But somewhere along the way, he decided he didn't like who he was being with that attitude. He chose to look for ways to help the people in the association. He uncovered ways he could be of service.

As part of being a person that gave, he served on the board during a tense time for the association. He boldly stood by the side of his leader through a troubled matter. Later, the president had a referral opportunity come to her. She enthusiastically recommended the professional that stood by her side and was always willing to help.

The work not only went to this service-minded individual but was the very thing that launched his career. Years later, he discovered that most of his work could be tracked to that incident in one way or another.

Apply the Giving and Receiving Principle to Your Customers

Giving the client a little extra over what they were expecting can create a positive impression and develop long-term loyalty. There is a balance to this, though. You don't want to go so far that you overgive and it hurts you. It is a dance between the two, but if you find the balance, it will be worth your effort.

The balance is not just about doing something extra that will delight your customer but also about who you are as a brand. According to Accenture Strategic Research Report, 42 percent of American consumers will walk away from a company that they don't agree with their actions and values.[8]

When a business owner is thinking of ways to give to their clientele, it is important that they reflect the company values and also stay in alignment with the demographic the business serves. Focusing on the right customer demographics and matching their values has become more important in the past couple of years since the millennials have taken over the workplace.

With the influx of millennials dominating the workforce starting in 2016, the business front and values have shifted. The demand for

---

[8] J. Vredenburg, S. Kapitan, A. Spry, and J.A. Kemper. 2020. December 5, 2018. "Brands Taking a Stand: Authentic Brand Activism or Woke Washing?," *Journal of Public Policy & Marketing* 39, 074391562094735. doi.org//10.1177/0743915620947359. www.accenture.com. https://journals.sagepub.com/doi/abs/10.1177/0743915620947359?journalCode=ppoa.

authenticity is strong; look of websites and graphics have dramatically changed and so has the importance of social media with more emphasis on being an influencer and equality.

Also, according to 60 Years Catalyst, in the United States, the millennials compose of a more diverse population. *Harvard Business Review* article by Avivah Wittenberg-Cox declares more women are entering the workforce than ever before which will have a dramatic impact on sales, marketing, and how business is done.[9]

When looking to give a little more, think outside of the box. Search for the little things can make all the difference. This can vary widely from sending a text of encouragement to passing on information that would really benefit them.

Application Corner

Exercise #1: Strengthen Your Receiving Muscles

Daily, look for ways to receive support that people offer and accept it. If someone gestures to let you be first in line, thank them and take the spot. If someone gives you a suggestion, thank them and recognize their intention to help you whether you use their advice or not. If someone likes your social media post, let their support sink in and grow used to that feeling of being supported.

Exercise #2: Pop Quiz on Your Receiving Ability

When was the last time you assisted someone in business for no reason? Write down who, when, and what you did.

If the time was longer than two weeks ago, it is time to assist. Plant seeds of good will. Trust what you send out will come back. How it returns often is unexpected so letting go of expectations is encouraged.

---

[9] "Generations: Demographic Trends in Population and Workforce." March 2, 2021. www.catalyst.org. www.catalyst.org/research/generations-demographic-trends-in-population-and-workforce/.

Exercise #3: Client's Demographic Sneak Peek

Evaluate your clients' demographics.

What are their highest values?

What are their greatest concerns?

What little things can you do that will make a difference to them?

This can vary widely from doing things like responding quickly to their needs and celebrating their wins to recognizing their birthdays or retweeting one of their posts. Get creative.

Mistake #14: Didn't Set Up Expectations Appropriately for Self, Employees, and Customers

Expectations are tricky and have gotten more than one small business owner in trouble. When the standard is too high, it can be impossible to meet and creates discouragement. If the promises aren't met that leads to dissatisfied clients. This has the potential for burnout. It can also result in a deep-seeded resentment either toward ourselves or the people we are working with or both.

If the standards are not high enough, that creates chaos and uninspired working conditions, and your potential isn't met. That produces resentment. Plus, clients will leave more often to work with other places that have higher standards.

How do you set up the conditions that will work for you, your staff, and your clients? Expectations need to be set in the sweet spot of being achievable—not too hard and not too easy. The perfect balance happens when expectations causes a person to stretch, inspire, and grow at a comfortable, doable pace. A speed that keeps them a bit nervous, without hindering your peak performance.[10]

It is important to know that the efforts put in are valuable. Plus, everyone needs to know exactly what is expected and how to know if they are meeting those expectations.

Expectations of Self

A lot of times business owners have unspoken expectations of themselves. For instance, they feel like they need to bring in a specific amount of money into the business in the first week, month, or year. Or look a certain way, present a certain way, or connect with certain people by a certain time.

Suppose you are one of those that falls into the high expectations of the results you produce in a short amount of time. In that case, you are

---

[10] I. Fisic. March 11, 2022. "Why and How to Create Performance Standards in an Organization (plus Examples)," *Clockify Blog*. https://clockify.me/blog/author/ivana-fisic/.

more likely to experience anxiety and overwhelm. The one thing that is guaranteed in the business world is the unexpected. Maybe, it will take you longer to make your sale and maybe the work you sent out to be done will be delayed. Maybe, a global disease will sweep the planet and change the whole nature of doing things. Whatever it is, there will be unexpected obstacles thrown at you. Suppose you measure the quality of your work by unrealistic markers. In that case, it will be hard to feel positive about what you are doing.

On the other hand, there are those entrepreneurs whose expectations are too low. For example, "I am going to spend the next quarter researching my market so I have a better idea of what is out there." That sounds reasonable. But when you consider that business is about making money to support at least yourself, taking an entire quarter to only be researching and not bring in any income is not sustainable. It is missing out on the learning that comes from being in the game of prospecting.

The low expectations can also sound like—"I need to get my website perfect before I do any sales," or "get the brochure done," or, or, or. Stop already. Many of my clients have had this "I need to ... first" syndrome when we started working together. When they stop that and place sales as the priority, they feel better with the money coming in. By being in the game of meeting with prospects and learning what their concerns are and where they are getting tripped up, you will glean valuable information about your niche.

The balance is not a one-time thing either. When balancing our expectations of ourselves, it is important to take in the whole picture of where we are currently at and to hold ourselves accountable to the objectives. I have had clients upset that they weren't achieving a certain level of productivity that they were accustomed to hitting.

When we looked at what was going on, they had dealt with many personal and family issues during that time. It was unrealistic for them to expect to be achieving at the same level with the added complication of an emotionally exhausting situation. Sometimes to set expectations, compassion is needed. If the owner is too hard on themselves, it will zap their motivation to keep going.

The behavior of being too hard on ourselves can often happen because fear is driving us.[11] To better cope with fear, implementing a practice (mindfulness, meditation, yoga, breath work) that releases these emotions can be helpful. That will allow us to approach our work from a place of calm and centeredness.

Mindset Play

Playing with mindset can be a fun exploration on how we approach our expectations. One way you can play with mindset is to determine what kind of energy or quality would be most productive to have before you do a task. Or, in other words, what attribute do you need to become the person who has accomplished the goal you are going for?

For example, if you are about to attend a networking group, you might determine that showing up with magnetism might draw people to you. If that is the quality you want to be, have, or exhibit breathe into that quality before you walk into the meeting or click the join button online. Feel yourself tap into that essence of magnetism. How that does that feel in your body?

At the end of the day, track how it went. How many people did you speak to? Did you speak to more people because that is what a magnetic person would do? Did you reach out to others and ask for a connection because that is what a magnetic person would do?

My approach is the night before each workday I determine three mindsets that would best serve the tasks of the upcoming day. I might pick the qualities based on the events or I might sense that a certain feeling would be supportive to perform at my best.

There are days I want to gain more traction on a certain goal. That day I might pick productivity. Another day when I have been going hard for a long time, I might want the day to feel restorative.

Other days, it might benefit me to embody a different quality. I look at the quarterly objectives and think: Who do I need to become to reach that objective? Often, I pick the quality of being a warrior. To me, a

---

[11] M. Tartakovsky. November 4, 2017. "5 Suggestions for Setting Realistic Expectations for Yourself," *Psych Central.* https://psychcentral.com/blog/5-suggestions-for-setting-realistic-expectations-with-yourself#3.

warrior gets the job done and doesn't second guess or hesitate. For a lot of things on my list, such as prospecting, I would hesitate if I didn't commit myself to just write the e-mail or pick up the phone.

Don't necessarily use the qualities I picked for me. Pick the qualities that you want to grow into and aspire to or would most support you. This experiment will be of most service if the qualities resonate with you.

At the end of the week, track the progress you have made toward your weekly goals. Compare the results you were able to achieve doing this focus exercise verses when you didn't. You will be able to see if this type of practice will increase your results and if it would be supportive to make into a daily habit.

Expectations of Others

The business owner's responsibility is to set up proper expectations at the beginning of the working relationship with a client. This can be tricky because the customer might be coming in with unspoken expectations that they don't mention and will become upset when those unspoken standards are not met.

One way to avoid having these misunderstandings is to put the expectations into writing. This will vary on how to do this depending on the type of business you are running. For consultants, speakers, coaches, a great way to do this is to become extremely clear in the contract that your client signs during the onboarding process.

In the contract, it is best to outline what is the client's responsibility and what is yours. I even put in mine that it is the client's responsibility to let me know if something isn't working. Putting that in the contract sets the tone of the type of relationship I want to have with them. I want them to feel safe to speak up. I also want to trust that they will.

Money is another tricky issue that comes with expectations. From my experience of working with hundreds of clients, things go more smoothly the clearer you are about payment.

- What is the full price of the service?
- When are the payment dates?
- What happens if the payment is not met?

When I first started coaching, many of my coaching colleagues would invoice every month and wait for the check to come in the mail. This was a recipe for a lot of stress and pain for the practitioner trying to get paid.

Making the payment process as smooth as possible is the best policy. Also having a clear policy on how to handle concerns manages expectations.

I once worked with a company that hide their refund policy in the long terms and conditions legal jargon the clients signed. The hidden wording stated that there would be no refund for any reason. The price of the product was high ticket. The clients who were dissatisfied with the service and asked for a refund were upset about this form of treatment. I also was upset by the practice and cut off my affiliation.

Being upfront about how the money is handled is a best business practice. If you have a program or product that offers a money back guarantee, do not hide the terms and conditions. The more upfront about you refund policy the better. If there is a time limit to the guarantee, make sure that date is mentioned in the contract several times or throughout your program.

If you are offering an online signature product, put in print and on video what the customer needs to do to qualify for that guarantee. Be as specific as you can. In some programs, they will spell out what homework assignments need to be completed and by when. Repetition is your friend on making sure the terms and conditions are clear to your client to limit the confusion.

Boundaries With Clients

Since I have worked as an entrepreneur, well forever, it wasn't until I started teaching did I learn what a perk it was being self-employed. Being an entrepreneur gives us the freedom to pick who we worked with. If I didn't think someone was a match as a client, I never signed them on. If we got going and it wasn't working (rarely did this happen), I would refer them to a better fit. When I first started teaching, I was slapped with the reality that I couldn't pick who would be my student, and second, I couldn't fire the problematic students.

Ok, I admit it, I would recruit from my 101 class my favorite students for 102 so I guess in that way I did pick who I taught. My 102 class would be filled with my former students and those classes were a lot of fun because they knew how I taught, trained the newcomers, and picked me as their teacher so they wanted to be there.

But to the students I wasn't a good fit for, if they didn't opt to resign from my course, we were stuck together for sixteen weeks. That wasn't a problem for most students, but for the occasional one, that reality created bumps for both of us. For most semesters, there were one or two students out of a hundred whose behavior escalated to the point that it wasn't acceptable.

As a new teacher, I was at a loss until I talked to my supervisor. I was extremely fortunate to have the best supervisor ever. She was seasoned and used to dealing with the various issues. She would guide me with the best practices that deal with the situation from students threating violence with other students and me, racism, students showing up to class stoned, to make up policies for those who were in out of jail during the semester, to how to support the homeless students, and those dealing with suicidal tendencies, plus a host of other family issues that would show up in class. There wasn't one situation that I approached her with that she hadn't experience before and knew the best way to handle it.

The second guideline that was at my disposal and one that my supervisor guided me too was the college's Code of Conduct manual. In that manual, it stated the expected behavior of the student and if that wasn't met, the process that would unfold. I learned as a teacher to appreciate the Code of Conduct. Having that manual and the college having strict guidelines of what was appropriate so everyone could have a safe learning environment was critical for everyone to have a chance at getting an education.

When the class behavior escalated, I had that Code of Conduct to help the student understand what was acceptable in class and what wasn't. I only had to refer to it once privately to a student. That Code provided a safety net for me as a teacher and it gave me the power to keep the learning environment one where all students could learn in. It was the enforcer of boundaries of what would and would not happen in the classroom holding both me and the students accountable to be respectful.

In business, we don't naturally have a code of conduct manual or behavioral expectations unless we consciously create them. Putting similar safety nets in our business is critical to keep us as business owners safe and keep our clients safe. Best practices are to have a Code of Conduct for your employees, employer, and sometimes for the customers, too. This is a worthwhile practice to have even if you are a solopreneur.

Working with mentors and business lawyers can be extremely helpful in learning the best practices. Even if you know what to do, talking to a mentor who has been there and asking how to address the situation ethically can be really helpful and keep the business owner out of hot water.

Taking ethic classes in your industry will raise your awareness of the ethical and moral issues that can rise in a business setting. Knowing what the best practices are and the professional standards that must be met, and how an organization needs to function is critical.

Many industries with changing laws and guidelines require the practitioner to take continuing education to stay on top of those changes. I have worked with clients who were unaware of some of the industry standards and did some behavior that landed them in court. Their unintentional actions put them at risk to lose their license and serve possible jail time.

Expectations of Clients

Clients have expectations of those they are working with.

The common ones:

- The business they are working with will listens to them.
- The company has the ability to determine the problem and reference ideas on how to fix it.
- The business will use best practices to solve problems that they are hired for.
- The business will use processes that have value and are up to date.
- The business will apply a personal touch[12] when possible.

---

[12] "8 Client Expectations from a Market Research Firm." February 20, 2014. *Market Research Firm Syracuse NY.* https://rmsresults.com/2014/02/20/8-client-expectations-from-a-market-research-firm/.

Application Corner

Exercise #1: Sweet Spot of Expectations

Look for the sweet spot of your expectations. This is something you can monitor and tweak during your CEO meetings.

Important things to track:

- What is your expectation for your work performance?
- What is working?
- What isn't working?
- Is there a different way to achieve the same result faster?
- How much is mindset affecting your result?
- If you were going use self-compassion with your work, how would you approach your work differently?

Exercise #2: Payment Expectations

Some areas to consider around payment expectations:

- What is your policy if the client is late? Repeatedly late?
- Do you offer a refund?
- If you offer a guarantee, what are the terms? How can you track if the terms are met?
- If there is a dispute, how will it be handled?
- Is the price by hour or fixed? If it is fixed what is included in that price and what items would be considered additional? Is the additional items and the price for those services included in the contract?
- Have you made room in the agreement for things to go wrong? How will things be handled if the unexpected occurs?
- Before you begin work, have you provided the context how you work and what the process will look like?
- Do you have a system of handling questions and concerns?
- Do you make a habit to say no to potential clients that would be a poor fit from the start? If the working conditions become unacceptable, do you have a process to handle offloading the agreement?

Exercise #3: Value-Based Code of Conduct

Write a values-based Code of Conduct that aligns with your mission statement.

Exercise #4: What Are Your Boundaries?

What are your expectations with your clients?

- What are your boundaries?
- What are you as a business owner willing to put up with?
- What will you not?
- How will you communicate when it is not working?
- How well do you know the ethical guidelines and rules in your industry?
- What safety net do you have in place in case you are in a situation that is outside the scope of your work?

For example, in my contract, I make it clear that I can consult with other experts in the mental health field if I become aware of a life-threatening situation or if illegal behavior has occurred such as abuse to a minor.

Expectations can run the gambit from the standards you run your business by to how well the relationship goes with yourself, your employees and contractors, your clients, and the general public.

Four Core Principles Every Business Expert Wishes They Knew From the Start

CHAPTER 5

Transform Into a Business Growing Machine

When an entrepreneur starts down the path of building their business, the one guarantee is they will make mistakes. As one of my business mentors used to always say, success leaves clues. By learning about those clues and what core principles underlie successful businesses can save the owner from a lot of hiccups.

Let's dive in and see the fundamentals that every business expert wishes they had known from the start.

Core Principle #1: Secret Weapon of Responsibility

My profession demands excellence in every minute detail, 100 percent honesty, precision, and accountability. Not only do I need to be accountable, but I need to ensure my employees are, too. With each patient, we must achieve rapport and open honest communication. This is essential. Lives are at stake. This means my entire staff and I must verify, verify, verify. To do this, I have found it is critical to be 100 percent open, honest, and precise.

—Dr. Rheim Jones, Board Certified Orthopedic Surgeon
Founder of Teton Medical Center

Entrepreneurs who take on responsibility for everything in their business achieve more success.[1] This doesn't mean that the entrepreneur does all the work, but they oversee the results and the work that is being done. If something is not functioning in their business, they do what is

---

[1] P. Shallard. n.d. "Why Taking Responsibility for Everything Is the Entrepreneur Secret Weapon." www.petershallard.com/ (accessed April 19, 2022).

necessary to find a solution. One of the main reasons taking responsibility for what is happening in the business is a good policy because it keeps the owner hunting for solutions.

There is a fine balance with taking responsibility. If you take on too much pressure, you can be immobilized. If you don't take enough, it causes business growth to be stagnant or go backward. The trick is to take on the responsibility and believe that you can do something about it.

Keeping a growth mindset versus a fixed mindset can make all the difference. Having a growth mindset means you believe there is something you can do about it. A fixed mindset is believing you as a person is flawed, and there is nothing you can do to fix it. Part of the growth mindset understands that errors happen. Mistakes are inevitable. It is what we do when we make those mistakes that make all the difference. First off, there is no clear guide on how to be successful. Each success story and road map to building business is different. Still, each successful business has goofed up in the past and will do it again in the future. That is consistency that can be counted on.

The key determining factor on whether a business will grow and rebound is how the entrepreneur responds when something isn't working. The best way is to recognize the error and then take actions to course correct, and uncover out a better way to respond. To correct the mistakes, it might require investigation to figure out exactly what was the root cause that produced the current results. This isn't always easy to determine but worth it.

Dr. Jones decided to launch his own business as a surgeon and build a knee center. It is clear in his quote that as an entrepreneur he took every aspect of his business seriously and put in every possible measure that he could to guarantee there wouldn't be misunderstandings. He didn't take lightly any part of his business. Lives were at stake. The price was too high for him to take errors lightly. This high standard was the bedrock of his extremely successful practice.

A major part of being responsible in business is to analyze and pay attention to how you make decisions and how they affect the outcomes. The best decision making in the ever-changing work environment is not always simple. The disadvantage of working only with your instincts is that sense is limited to what that person is aware of. Instinct can only operate on what it has access to. It lacks the information that comes from the data and the insight that comes from tracking trends, new and current realities, and the evolutionary nature of the work environment.

But to not have intuition be part of the decision-making process would certainly be limiting and often dramatically harmful to the process. From the psychologist Sooalu and his colleagues' research, they were able to determine that there is a gut, brain, and heart correlation to decision making. In other studies, the psychologist found the soul's involvement in making decisions, also.

Sooalu stated that the brain uses adaptive neural network when making a decision. The brain refers our ability to use analytical and cognitive thinking. For the heart, they referred to the emotional and affective response. And for the gut, it refers to any involvement of intuition. They found that there is a solid connection of all three to decision making.

Fifty-two percent of the respondents did not accurately predict which of the three ways would be dominant in the how they made decisions. The researchers suggested better decisions to raise awareness of your preferred bias.[2]

This research taps into the "feeling versus thinking" argument. Turns out both are important, and if you prefer one side, you need to implement more of the other side. No matter which way you default in making decisions—head, heart, or gut—when it comes to business, assessing all the resources available to make the best decision at the moment is critical. That is where the power of the microdecision-making technique comes in. It incorporates both instinct and analysis.

The concept of the microdecision is to make the smallest choice possible to move forward. Taking a small step toward the goal gives time to test out your theory, gather information, see patterns, and receive feedback. That informs the next microdecision.

---

[2] G. Sooalu, S. Henwood, and A. Deo. March 18, 2019. "Head, Heart, and Gut in Decision Making: Development of a Multiple Brain Preference Questionnaire," *Sage Journals*. https://Journals.sagepub.com/. https://journals.sagepub.com/doi/full/10.1177/2158244019837439.

The power of the microdecision limits the tendency that some business owners have toward striving for the perfect choice.[3] It is impossible to find the perfect choice with the endless number of options available to an entrepreneur. Being stuck in perfectionism can paralyze the decision-making process.

There is value when making a decision to separate it into its various components. It is common for us to collapse a whole bunch of parts together. When this happens, it is best to pull apart the different sections that make up the choice. Being clear on all the components helps make the choice feel less overwhelming. Some components may be financial, others strategic, often emotional or mindset, come into play resulting in conflicting values. When we see each part, it is easier to grasp the overall picture.

We can focus on each chunk of the decision and weigh the pros and cons. Most of the time when the values at play are brought to light, relief comes to the person making the decision. They know what is most important to them, and they immediately gain clarity to move forward.

If the owner suffers from perfectionistic tendencies, they have another step to take: giving up the idea of a perfect solution and finding satisfaction with good enough.

All this sounds extremely simplistic when making high-stake decisions. There are times in business when you will be confronted with so many moving parts and most of them are unknown, it can become challenging. It is helpful to separate what you have control over with what you don't and give yourself grace in what you choose, knowing that you did the best you could with what you knew at the time.

The Higher Risk That Comes With Age

Decisions can become harder when there is a perception of there being more at risk. Many older entrepreneurs I spoke with mentioned how much more difficult it was to make choices when the desire for retirement loomed ahead. They stated that it would be harder to bounce back because

---

[3] E. Bonabeau. May 2003. "Don't Trust Your Gut." https://hbr.org/. https://hbr .org/2003/05/dont-trust-your-gut.

more people depended on them and because of their close proximity to retirement age. Many of the entrepreneurs who were 50 and above mentioned being given less of a chance because of age discrimination.

In her article "How to Make a High Stakes Decision," Amy Gallo argues that there is a balance in decision making. The tension is between taking too much time to make the choice and, on the other side, rushing it. She claims that a high-stake decision shouldn't be made by oneself. She also warns about the dangers of being biased. She points out that our first impression may or may not be right, but we all have attachment toward our best interest. We all start with an inclination that can have an unconscious influence if we aren't careful. It is best to not make a decision alone and to gather more information. Bias shows up in our decision-making process when we prejudge how to approach the decision. It takes work to be open to the process and to not only consider our point of view.[4]

The Foundation Skill to Thrive in Business

With the rate and speed that commerce moves, it becomes absolutely critical for the owner to daily take time to assess the most important actions to propel them forward. The best way to build a thriving company is to have a habit of taking action. It is a choice to become a master of action and learn what it takes no matter what the obstacles, whether they come from children, spouses, ex-spouses, parents, friends, and ourselves, or natural obstacles that come with owning a business and being human. It's a skill set to move forward supporting our values, both at work and personal life.

You can have access to all of the most powerful and transformational information in the world, but it is *not* until you are able to really master this ability of transforming knowledge into action, that you will see your business explode.

To do this tracking what is working and what isn't is a fundamental step. It can make the difference between whether you win or not. By tracking your actions, you can quickly discover your patterns, what to do

---

[4] A. Gallo. August 12, 2015. "How to Make a High-Stakes Decision," *Harvard Business Review.* https://hbr.org/2011/05/how-to-make-a-high-stakes-decision.

more of, and what continually gets in the way. This information is golden. With it, you can make more of the right decisions at the right time.

It is just too easy to become caught up in the train of "I have so much to do that I can't find time to think about the overall view of my business." This is a serious mistake. Entrepreneurs can't afford *not* to stop and reevaluate and gain the perspective to make sure they are heading where they want to go and that they are doing it the most effectively.

What Hidden Magic Can Be Found in Asking Radical Business Questions?

Another place to track is the questions you ask of yourself and of your work. Consider if they are radical enough. Are you asking far-out questions that might look a bit out there?

A radical question I once asked that got people looking at me like I was crazy was: What could I do to make my house pay for itself?

That idea floated around until the thought came, what would happen if I had seminars in my basement? Holding them at hotels was expensive. My basement is not as professional as a hotel, but I was just starting out at that time, so I gave it a try.

The first workshop I held out of my house was called *Supercharge Your New Year.* To my surprise, my mother joined. At that time, my mother was at risk of losing her home. She needed a job. In the first workshop held in my basement, she declared that was what she was going to get. Her sister was at the workshop too. (Ok, family support is a great thing.)

My mom and her sister had this rivalry going ... well, their whole life. They started competing about who would do more to reach their goals.

Long story short, my mom applied for the job to not be outdone by her sister. She was hired and became the top salesperson in the first month. Two years later, she married her boss.

Boom. My radical question saved my mom and me from the misery of living together, which led to my mom finding true love.

Victory on both our parts.

When thinking about the type of questions that you are asking, Jessica H. Lawrence the former CEO of Girl Scouts of San Gorgonio Council, warns the pressure to complete a project or get something done might influence how we ask questions. This tendency to be in a hurry has the risk of approaching the questions in a transactional nature that leaves out the human element. When we don't explore the personal side of what is happening, we will not understand motivations and where the resistance or blocks are coming from.

Lawrence claims that radical questions are open-ended and are more feeling-based than fact-based.[5] I would argue that there are different types of radical questions. The type like what I asked when exploring how to make my house pay for itself—questions that hopefully provoke innovation. The other types that are more focused on understanding the human element to the problem like what Lawrence was commenting on.

Application Corner

Exercise #1: Compelling Your Business Forward Daily

Have you ever worked hard all day long and then wondered what you had accomplished at the end of the day? What kept you from getting the important things done?

If you set your priorities daily, create a form of accountability that keeps you motivated, and track your actions throughout a day, you'll spend little time wondering if you are spinning your wheels and lot more attention will be going to meeting your objectives.

To make sure that you are moving your business forward, break down your big objective for the quarter into daily action steps.

- Ask yourself, which three steps do I need to take today to get me closer to the big quarterly goal?
- Write down those steps.
- Post it you so you see them throughout the day.
- Implement a system that holds you accountable for what you actually do. There are many options, from using your smartphone or Google Docs to Post-it notes or accountability buddies.

---

[5] J.H. Lawrence. June 27, 2015. "The Practical Business Radical: Asking More Powerful Questions at Work," *Press Enterprise*. www.pe.com/2015/06/27/the-practical-business-radical-asking-more-powerful-questions-at-work/.

- At the end of the day, track what you accomplished and what you didn't.

Exercise #2: Possible Metrics to Track

Some metrics to pay attention to. There most likely will be more things to add to the list depending on your business.

Time

1. How much time is going to what action? Break it down into subject headings and clock yourself. For example, marketing, copywriting, website maintenance, sell calls, product development, product delivery, and whatever else you spend time on.
2. Track your downtime and your reset and restorative moments throughout the day.
3. Record how many times you laughed during the day. This is important to make sure that your brain is receiving dopamine hits that help you to perform better.
4. Which actions achieve the biggest results?
5. What actions were giving you the happiness at doing? Which ones drained you?

Business Relationships

1. Who are your referral partners?
   How often do you reach out to them?
   Do you have a system to stay in contact with them at least every 90 days?
   What ways do you give benefit to your referral partners?
   Do you know who your top partners are?
2. Are you staying on top of your relationships with your employees and contractors?
   How is their level of performance? How do you measure it?
   How is your relationship with your business colleagues and associates?
   Where is the biggest area of friction? What part of the relationship is working the best?

Clients/Customers

- What percentage of your customers is repeat?
- Are you staying in contact with your former customers?
- How much is your customer acquisition costs?
- What is your average retention length of a client?
- What is your lifetime value of a client?
- Where did your best customers come from?

Level of Stress

- What is your happiness level at work?
- What stresses you?
- What lessens the stress?

CEO Meetings

- How often are you having CEO meetings?
- How is the profit margin?
- Do you know what this quarter's objectives are? Do you know where you are in achieving them?
- What would make your CEO meetings more productive?
- What are the radical questions that you could ask at the meeting?
- Are you reviewing the company's vision weekly?

Resources

Parsons, N. February 15, 2022. "17 Key Business Metrics You Should Track to Find Success." *LivePlan Blog.* www.liveplan.com/blog/what-startup-metrics-should-i-track/.

Schröder, C.A. September 18, 2018. "Assuming Responsibility—A Key Trait for Successful Entrepreneurs." https://schroederca.medium.com/. https://schroederca.medium.com/assuming-responsibility-35e270d1584f

Shallard, P. n.d. "Why Taking Responsibility for Everything Is the Entrepreneur Secret Weapon." www.petershallard.com/. www.petershallard.com/taking-responsibility-for-everything-is-the-entrepreneur-secret-weapon/ (accessed May 5, 2022).

Core #2: Stay in Momentum

Action is the foundational key to all success.

—Pablo Picasso

My biggest business mistake was not getting around to what I should have been doing. In the beginning, I kept waiting to take action because I felt like I didn't have all the expertise I needed. I wasn't ready. I didn't have a website. I was honing my skills...the list goes on.

It turns out no one is perfect, and how do we ever get better if we don't jump in feet first and get to work? Once I believed in myself and had confidence, the rest fell into place. I figured out I could work on the website, marketing, etc., along the way.

No one starts off 100 percent ready and has everything in top shape. I finally learned that I had to just get started, and it's amazing what happened afterward. As the weeks went by, which turned into years, it was important to keep putting one foot in front of the other and employing myself regularly. My results exceeded my expectations, and I've reached levels that I thought would take a lot longer than they have by just getting started.

Just take action!

—Brieonna Aljets, Managing Broker and Trainer

When my seventh child was two years old, she loved to play puzzle games on the iPhone. Every time she put the puzzle together, she clapped her hands together and called out, "I did it. I did it. Yeah! I did it!"

How much better would we be as adults if we learned to celebrate our little successes like my two-year-old? You make a call that you have been dreading or have that difficult conversation with someone, and once you finish, you say, "I did it! Yeah, I did it." How much more motivated would you be to do more challenging things on your desk?

Celebrate your successes. The small ones, even if it is a phone call or you showed up on time for the first time in a month. These little celebrations are important in keeping you motivated. No one wants to keep working if there is no reward. Positive psychology has found that honoring the little wins keeps a person engaged and moving forward. Little wins release neurotransmitter dopamine or the "feel good" drug.[6]

Keep the Momentum With the Magic of Accountability

The old adage is what you track grows. The truth is what you track *in front of others* accelerates your results. Something happens when you are in a collective where everyone in the group is striving toward similar things. There is power with others that doesn't happen when you are alone. Sometimes you hear something that another person is doing, which will spark an idea.[7]

When people hear about a business practice from a different industry, they can be inspired. This makes their work fresher and stands out.

Other times, it will remind you of something that might be good to pay attention to. For example, I often show up to an online group where everyone writes. At the beginning of our gathering, each person takes their turn to say in front of the rest of the group what they are going to do for the next hour in our co-working session.

One night someone mentioned how tired they were. That comment made me realize I was also tired, which led me to rethink what I would work on. I decided instead of doing the project that was going to require a lot of mental heavy lifting, I would save that for the early morning the next day when I was at my best. Instead, I would do a different task that needed to be done but didn't require as much mental output.

The result was I completed the task, and then the next day, I was able to show up to the heavy lifting project without the pressure of needing to make it to the other task too.

---

[6] T.M. Amabile and S.J. Kramer. May 6, 2020. "The Power of Small Wins," *Harvard Business Review.* https://Hbr.org/. https://hbr.org/2011/05/the-power-of-small-wins.

[7] A.L. Brownlee and S.J. Motowidlo. January 2011. "Effects of Accountability to Group Members and Outcome Interdependence ..." www.researchgate.net/ Publication. www.researchgate.net/publication/266232121.

Obviously, accountability also adds the bonus of having a deadline. I was once in an accountability group with many heavy hitters in the business world. We gathered for a few hours once a month and informed the others about our business and then the one project we hadn't gotten to because everything kept getting in the way. We explained the value that project would have to our business and to our clients. Then we committed to measurable action steps that we would take that coming month to move the project forward. The next time we met, we came with a report of what we did and proof that we actually did what we said we were going to do.

There was an additional part to the accountability. We each signed a contract that we would accomplish what we said we would do or we would pay $100 to the pot. What was in the pot would go to charity at the end of the year.

The game was on.

A funny thing happened as we played. Each of us quickly learned that we needed to be better at judging what could be accomplished in a month. If memory serves, each one of us had overstretched what we thought we could do the first month. Part of the reason we all did that, I believe, is we didn't want to look like slackers in front of our peers.

Most of us learned that we needed to have a head start on our goals so that we would not be burning the midnight oil the day before our meeting. Despite the intense pressure that came from committing to ambitious goals, no one held back. We all went for it. We made good on our commitments each month. Despite doing this month after month, our efforts didn't fade. Our goals didn't fade and neither did our support for each other.

Why? Most of us admitted after the year was done that none of us wanted to look like a slacker. What was the end result of the accountability group? All of us accomplished more in our business that year than we had ever done before.

The Power of Small Little Actions

According to James Clear in his foundational book *Atomic Habits*, he claims the way to achieving one's goals is through taking regular small actions. "Breakthrough moments are often the result of many previous actions, which build up the potential required to unleash a major change."

No magic pill for business success. Dang. Business success is a cumulative effect that builds momentum. Take those small steps over and over in a consistent fashion until you reach the tipping point where everything starts to work.

Makes sense, but the problem is many business owners give up too early and ditch their strategy to chase the newer shiny strategy, technique, or trend. The habit researcher Clear found that "habits often appear to make no difference until you cross a critical threshold."[8]

No one ever knows when they are going to cross that threshold, so how do you strengthen your commitment to keeping at it until you cross that finish line even when there is no proof that you will ever make it?

That's where commitment and grit come into play.

Refueling Motivation

One of the reasons business owners give up too early is that they don't see the pressure and frustration that is accumulating under the surface. To help with that, implementing a small business habit might do the trick in keeping you motivated.

What's that one habit you could put in place that would make all the difference in the outcomes that you are wanting to achieve? Maybe it could be cleaning your desk? That would put more organization into your work and reduce the time required to hunt for something. It would suggest to your subconscious that you are an organized person as you tackle the bigger tasks.

Libby Sander, in her article "The Case for Finally Cleaning Your Desk" published by *Harvard Business Review*, found in her research and those of her colleagues that a simple thing like a messy desk "significantly influence[s]" our thinking, feelings, and actions. In addition to that they found it impacts how we make decisions, and the ripple effect affects our relationships.[9]

---

[8] J. Clear. 2021. *Atomic Habits: Tiny Changes, Remarkable Results* (CELA), p. 20.

[9] L. Sander. March 29, 2019. "The Case for Finally Cleaning Your Desk," *Harvard Business Review*. https://Hbr.org. https://hbr.org/2019/03/the-case-for-finally-cleaning-your-desk?registration=success.

Apparently, our brains like order. A messy desk affects our ability to pay attention to the task in hand. Going on a five-to-ten-minute cleanup sprint daily could have an amazing impact on our environment. In fact, I tried doing that for 30 days and was shocked at how much order I was able to put into place in my home and work environments and how much better I felt tackling other tasks.

When I did those 10-minute sprints, I did them when I either felt sluggish or when I was feeling anxious that day. I would get up from my workstation and tackle the mess for only 10 minutes and whatever I got done I got done.

I made it into a game. How much could I get done in 10 minutes? Mark, get set, go. This game was more fun to play with others. I used to play it with my family when the children were young. "Many hands make light work" is true, and the sprints shifted their moods for the better.

Even if it is only me playing the game in those 10 minutes, not only did that one little spot I tackled become cleaner, but it shifted my emotions so that I would be reenergized to go back to work. I found that my performance level for the next hour was higher than it would have been if I hadn't done the cleaning sprint and kept at my job.

Sanders reported that having those little messes in our environment increases anxiety and procrastination behaviors. Maybe desk-cleaning sprints are not your thing. Perhaps a little habit that could be supportive of your overall motivation could be calling your leads before you do anything else? That is doing the hard thing first to get it over with.

Research found that the stress of delaying the hard tasks affects how you perform all your other assignments.[10] The dread of doing that one thing clouds our work performance which becomes problematic when considering we only have so much willpower available to us. This becomes a double-edged sword. The delay causes fatigue which feeds on the desire to delay even more.

For some people, a supportive habit might be as simple as showing up on time. (The benefits of that were covered in Mistake #3.) For others, it

---

[10] Jimmy. July 27, 2021. "Hardest or Easiest Work First? What the Research Shows," *The Productive Engineer*. https://Theproductiveengineer.net/. https://the-productiveengineer.net/hardest-or-easiest-work-first-what-the-research-shows/.

might be to complete a project before moving on to another. For another businessperson, it may require more awareness of how their communication style affects others so they can achieve smoother working relationships. For a deeper exploration on the power of a small habit can have and what type of habit can create signification change, read *Atomic Habits* by James Clear.

Doing something small that resets you and lets you have a little win builds up your motivation for your overall working experience.

Surge Capacity

Another thing that might be holding business owners back from staying in momentum is they might be suffering from surge capacity. When a crisis happens, there is a boost of energy to help us cope. But if the crisis goes on too long, that burst of energy becomes depleted.[11]

Suppose you are not continuously replenishing yourself. You will eventually experience waning energy that will cause motivation depletion, and if that becomes bad enough, burnout and depression set in.

To counter this downward spiral, it helps to be self-compassionate. Understand that there is a reason that you are feeling tired, irritable, and exhausted. Instead of shaming yourself for not being able to do more, realize that you have been running a long race, and it is time to go easier.

That might be hard to do but small actions can make a big difference. Start with compassion, increase your sleep, eat replenishing food, and then listen to your yearnings. For example, when a woman I know slips in this spot, all she longs to do is watch TV. She used to guilt herself for wasting her time. Now she sees it as a way to restore herself and knows that her energy will return after a day or two, then she goes back to work feeling revitalized.

For others, going into nature is restorative. For my husband, time alone in the garage is the magic ticket. For me, it's reading a novel. Do whatever recharges you and remember it will fill up the depletion faster if you stop and honor that longing.

---

[11] "Is Your 'Surge Capacity' Depleted?" August 31, 2020. www.wbrc.com. www .wbrc.com/2020/08/31/is-your-surge-capacity-depleted/.

Application Corner

Exercise: Accountability Group

If you want to add more accountability in your business, consider forming an accountability group.

- The first step is to determine who will be in the group. When and where will they meet?
- What will be the guideline and how will the group hold people accountable?
- Each member will then determine the individual objectives they want to meet and their deadline. Each person will list their big goal, and then the micro-goals that will progress toward the big goal.
- Set a firm date of when you will meet that microgoal.
- What are the consequences if the action steps aren't taken?
- What are the due dates for this sprint of microgoals?
- How will you report your results and prove your efforts?

Resource

Kou, C.Y. and V. Stewart. June 14, 2017. "Group Accountability: A Review and Extension of Existing Research." *Sage Journals.* https://Journals.sagepub .com/. https://journals.sagepub.com/doi/10.1177/1046496417712438.

CHAPTER 6

Building Powerful Relationships

Relationships in business connect the dots between all the moving parts. Even with the increase of articficial intelligence (AI) in our daily working life, it is people who program the AI and people who help forge the relationship between the various components of AI to talk to each other.

There are many different types of relationships in business. There are the relationships we have with ourselves, our environment, our customers or clients, our partners, our networks, our mentors, our colleagues, our suppliers, and our employees or contractors. Each of these relationships requires time, attention, and nurturing.

Core #3: Supportive Environments

Successful business owners set up their work environment to be supportive to them overall. They have systems put in place to keep the work flowing and not bogged down with irritants like hunting for a misplaced file. They also have items in their space that they find inspiring, uplifting, and motivating.

Not only are their work areas positive, but they also make sure the people they spend the most time with are positive and motivating. For example, when I want to pay more attention to my health, I go to a yoga center where the talk is about the latest organic eating program or the most recent outdoor adventure. When I want to make more money and grow my company, I seek out some of the world's best in business and spend time with them, either go through their trainings, watch their YouTube shows, or listen to their podcasts. Or I might read their books or talk with them in person or by video. I love to bathe myself in their thinking, processes, and how they look at life.

Seek out the people, groups, and activities that will support you and your company. Who you spend time with is a big part of how satisfied you will be with work. The other day I was talking with someone who was wanting to leave a job in order to honor a lifestyle that would be more supportive of their overall life. The one concern for this social butterfly was the isolation that they might experience by not being in a place buzzing with activity. They didn't want to miss the energy of an office.

"So, rent an office space filled with other entrepreneurs," I suggested. They hadn't thought of that nor had they explored the various ways they could ensure regular contact with others.

The beauty of being an entrepreneur is you get to design your work life to best suit you. Are you a social butterfly? Networking and a co-working office space might be the ticket for you. Prefer being introverted? Working from home might be ideal. Does a combination of being around people and having downtime keep you at your best—work from home and put in some virtual co-working sprints in place.

Bottom line: who you surround yourself with and how much time you spend with people dramatically affect your work life. If what you are currently doing isn't working, it doesn't take much to change it.

Competition and the Power of Being Stretched

Many entrepreneurs are competitive by nature. Being in a friendly competitive environment can be very supportive environment for the more competitive souls. One reason is when you are in a community where other people are committed and focused it is contagious.

I once was in a group that had a friendly contest tracking daily action steps. I was going along, just trying to do what I could. A few weeks into the contest, only men were at the top of the scoreboard. That lit a fire under me to have a female represented. I became superfocused and motivated to do more because of the competition.

Friendly competition helps entrepreneurs to get out of their own way.[1] Even if you don't think you are a competitive type, I have personally seen competition become a powerful motivator even for those who didn't

---

[1] F. Sines. January 17, 2019. "Encouraging Friendly Competition in Business." *Thrive Global.* https://thriveglobal.com/stories/encouraging-friendly-competition-in-business/#:~:text=Competition%20in%20the%20workplace%20can,challenges%20lead%20to%20professional%20growth.

think it would work for them. With the support of the group cheering them on, they couldn't help but be more driven.

The Power of Peer Mastermind Groups

Masterminds have been found to be powerful in providing the right environment for businesspeople. A mastermind is a group of peers who gather together to support each other's goals, hold each other accountable, and use the power of group think to compel each other forward.

Some of my best business connections and close friends have come out of mastermind groups. The concept of these types of groups became popular with Napoleon Hill's book *Think and Grow Rich*.

Why are mastermind groups so powerful? There are a lot of reasons, but some of them are obvious.

1. **Not feeling alone and feeling validated**

   I ran a virtual mastermind group with people from all over the country. Each person was in a different industry, but all of them were service-based. Every participant had been in business for over five years. The topic of the day was mindset.

   As each person admitted to struggling with a mindset issue an interesting thing happened, the other members relaxed as they listened to their colleagues explain their challenges. People spoke up that they had similar fears and concerns. The group naturally became tighter through seeing firsthand that they were not alone.

   As the mastermind members championed each other and brainstormed possible solutions, many reported: "It feels good to know I am not alone" and "If so and so has that challenge and they are good at X then maybe I can do it too."

   The group members left the meeting feeling inspired, understood, and motivated. They knew what they were going through was a shared experience and people were rooting for them.

2. **Being in a group that is cheering you on and reminding you to celebrate**

   What I love about being in a mastermind group, and running them, is how generous most participants are to each other. People who join mastermind groups come with an attitude to serve others and believe that similar support will come back to them.

Another by-product I experienced that I didn't expect was my fellow members recognized my growth and reflected that back to me, which was extremely valuable to gain a bigger picture of how far I had come. I have been able to do the same for them. Often, we as entrepreneurs are so in the game that we don't see the progress we are making. When growth is reflected to us, it rewards our brain that we are making progress. This leads to higher levels of motivation and ultimately higher levels of effort.

3. **Built in test market**

There is a lot of value in having people from different industries in a mastermind group. People in the same industry tend to look at a business situation with a similar lens. Having someone outside of the industry brings a fresh view to problem-solving and adds a broader perception of what is possible.

In my current mastermind, each of us brings the outline of our new programs and marketing to the group. Our meeting is the first place where we test our material. It is safe, we aren't judged, and everyone is honest. When I brought in a program I was putting together, I received feedback like "that is generic." And, "that sounds like all the other programs I have been seeing." When I hear feedback like that, I know I have missed the mark and need to dig deeper.

4. **Track successes**

One of the tricks for making a mastermind or a collective of colleagues be of value is knowing how to make the group work for you. Oftentimes, these groups have been set up to bring a business problem you are having to the collective and then the group will brainstorm solutions.

Most of the time, I know what to do in my business; I just need to do it. This is a similar spot for many people who have been in business for five or more years. For me going to a mastermind group to be told to do what I already know I need to do wouldn't be helpful. I need to be with other committed people to stay inspired and in the implementation zone and to answer my tech questions. That is the area I most often become stuck in.

Notice, how I took time to think about making the group work best for me as a whole. I also do it weekly before joining the call. Sometimes, that is a challenge. I will think over a few days about what to bring to the group that would best keep me moving forward. It helps me pay attention to my work life and what the snags are or what would be best serve me in my time in the meeting. It also aids the other members to know how to serve me in my allotted time. Meetings go best when each person is ready and not wondering around not knowing what they need or filling their time complaining about lacking clarity or everything that is going wrong.

5. **Improved work**

Most of our group members found that their work was at a higher quality since we would be showing it. This creates the power of peer pressure at its best.

6. **Power of the collective**

Better decisions are often made by the power of the collective. There is a group focus on solutions around the challenges and what obstacles might be coming that the person hadn't thought of.

Collective thinking gives a more comprehensive perception on the issue because each person in the group will be approaching it from different lenses and background training. For example, we have one person in the group who is an expert at technology and another person who is in management.

Their feedback comes from different business worlds and strengths. The tech person can easily solve tech issues while the person in management has been invaluable with how to navigate high-stake conversations and has amazing number of tips on how to negotiate higher prices.

We are also blessed to have people from all over the country and one from a different country. This gives us all a better understanding on national and international business trends and approaches.

7. **Deadlines**

Establishing deadlines to report the results to the group evokes the motivation to get something done. These regular accounting times measure what we have been able to accomplish between meetings.

I have tracked the results produced financially, the connections made, and my bold moves made when in this type of structure versus when I wasn't. The results were shocking. I made three times the amount of income and my networking relationships deepened. Even though I held myself accountable on my own, apparently, I go easier on myself than when others are looking.

The Scrum method was a revolutionary system that took the technology world by storm. They found accountability to be a critical part of their secret sauce. They advocate for teams to check in on their progress for no more than 15 minutes daily. This keeps the teams focused and productive.[2]

Do You Know What Conditions Inspire You to Jump in and Get Your Work Done?

On a coaching call, I encouraged a client to make her junk room a "room of inspiration." A place that was filled with things that inspired her. The goal was to go for 100 percent inspiration. That's right. A place that would light her up. And she did it. As a result, she had more fun in her life and became more productive.

"I didn't know that would make that much difference," she said.

Research shows that your environment affects your productivity.

How's Your Lighting Affecting You?

The lighting in your environment is part of the productivity equation. According to Anna Johansson from Enterpreneur.com: "Bright light, present on a regular basis, has been shown to make people happier, reducing both anxiety and depression."[3]

When I reflected on this research, I noticed that I didn't like working in my office and often would find other spots around the house. My office was dark, with two small windows to guard against the intense heat of

---

[2] J. Sutherland and J.V. Sutherland. 2014. *Scrum* (Currency).

[3] A. Johansson. November 14, 2018. "7 Ways Your Office Affects Productivity (Without Your Realizing It)," *Entrepreneur*. www.entrepreneur.com/article/322504.

desert summers. I had unconsciously gathered by windows with natural lighting. Now I consciously work by the windows in my home and turn on better lighting in my office.

What Color Is Perfect for You?

Another area to consider to make your environment more effective is the color of your walls. The1thing.com dove into the research of colors and tells us that blue has a calming effect that slows breathing and lowers blood pressure. Yellow creates energy, green is a relaxing hue, and orange picks up productivity.[4]

Which color will serve what you need? How fast can you have that wall painted or at least put a plant in your office with that color? If you have a green thumb, you might want to really consider putting in plants. According to American Society for Horticultural Science, article "The Effect of Live Plants and Window Views of Green Spaces on Employee Perceptions of Job Satisfaction" found "the presence of plants in the room helped reduced mental fatigue, increased attentiveness, lowered blood pressure, and increased productivity of participants."[5]

Does Hearing a Beat Help?

During COVID, my younger children were doing school online. Often, I heard the voices of teachers in the other room rambling on. "WHH-HAAA, whaaa, whaa."

Ugh. I finished school already and didn't want to go back. The answer? Stream Celtic music on my computer, allowing me to settle back into work.

---

[4] Team, The ONE Thing. June 7, 2016. "How These Colors Affect Your Productivity," *The ONE Thing*. www.the1thing.com/blog/the-one-thing/how-these-colors-affect-your-productivity/.

[5] A. Dravigne, T.M. Waliczek, R.D. Lineberger, and J. Zajicek. February 1, 2008. "The Effect of Live Plants and Window Views of Green Spaces on Employee Perceptions of Job Satisfaction." https://Journals.ashs.org/, (American Society for Horticultural Science). https://journals.ashs.org/hortsci/view/journals/hortsci/43/1/article.

How is noise affecting your productivity? Do you need background noise, silence, or music? Anna Johansson says research is not clear on if music makes you productive.[6] I say you know yourself best. Do more of what works for you.

If you are missing the noise of the coffee shop and can't be there, maybe stream white noise or if you want people around you, hop on a Meetup centered around working together. This is called body-doubling. Body-doubling is working on your task in the presence of another person. The rule is that the other people need to be present whether in person or online, working on a task with no talking. The theory behind it is this kind of activity keeps people focused and supports them to be resistant to distraction. The fact the other person is there serves as a form of accountability. Seeing other people staying on task for a certain amount of time is an active reminder to keep working.[7]

The environment can really affect your ability to be productive. According to Lindsay McGuire's article, "Workplace Productivity Statistics That Will Blow Your Mind," 71 percent of people said listening to music made them more productive."[8]

How Entrepreneurs Can Tap Into the Hidden Magic of a Simple Phrase

Establishing a supportive mental environment is just as important as a physical one. Sometimes entrepreneurs know what to do but just aren't doing it. Some say they aren't doing it because they have this overwhelming sense of fear. So, what do you do when you're blocked or aren't doing what you need to do to move forward?

---

[6] A. Johansson. November 14, 2018. "7 Ways Your Office Affects Productivity (Without Your Realizing It)," *Entrepreneur*. www.entrepreneur.com/article/322504.

[7] S. Panecasio. May 11, 2022. "The Productivity Hack That's Taking Over Tik-Tok," *CNET*. www.cnet.com/. www.cnet.com/culture/internet/the-productivity-hack-thats-taking-over-tiktok/.

[8] L. McFuire. n.d. "Workplace Productivity Statistics That Will Blow Your Mind," *Formstack Blog*. www.formstack.com/resources/blog-workplace-productivity-statistics.

There's a secret tool that's simple, can be very powerful, and can help you move from being frozen to rocking it. Before you can use this tool, you need to know what you're getting stuck on both externally and internally. Maybe it is that you are overwhelmed? Or are you afraid to fail again? Or...?

Once you become clear on what is causing you to be stuck, tune in to the type of feeling you want to have to move forward. If you can't figure that out, it's ok. Just pay attention to what it feels like right at the moment.

After you are clear on what might be stopping you, it is time to go on a hunt for a mantra—a short phrase—that you believe would move you forward. For example, I talked to a woman the other day who was dealing with chronic health issues. The doctor told her she needed to de-stress. At the same time, she also needed to rebrand her business and move into a better place career wise to support her family. She was stuck in the conflicting demands.

She wondered if it was possible for her to de-stress and still grow her business, even though it sounded impossible. Since we knew what she wanted to achieve more growth in her work and ease with her health, we explored a mantra that might work.

We compiled a list.

(Hint: You can Google a list of mantras or ask AI. There are tons.)

Finally, the mantra that resonated for her the most was: "I can. And I will."

As she spoke her mantra out loud every day, things shifted for her. She managed her energy and grew her business while staying in supportive energy.

By telling herself, "I can. And I will," she eased into tasks all through the day, her heart rate lowered, and her business bloomed. She moved ahead, despite the contradiction in her goals, by working with a mantra and focusing on her energy.

Years ago, a family member felt like he had too much to do. He couldn't keep up and didn't have time to do the things he wanted to accomplish. I wrote on a Post-it note: "I always make time for the most important things." I posted it on his bathroom mirror.

He thought it was a bunch of hocus-pocus, but he started doing the things he thought he didn't have the time for within the next couple of weeks of that Post-it note going up.

Application Corner

Exercise: Productivity Environment

Think about your environment. What slight changes can you make so it is more supportive?

For example: I bought myself some gloves with open fingers, so I can write in my living room without cold fingers during the winter months.

What slight change can you make to be more effective in your physical environment? For example a clean desk, a plant, or maybe work by a window.

What slight change can you make to be more effective with work lighting?

For example, move your desk to be closer to a window. Purchase a ring light.

What slight change can you make to be more effective with the noises you surround yourself with?

For example, stream music, wear noise canceling headphones, work at a library to be away from the home noise.

Core #4: Supercharged Networking and Mentorship

For most businesses, networking is one of the best ways to build. Networking smart in the limited time you have is critical. It comes down to knowing who your ideal client is and where they like to go, then going where they gather in large numbers. For some businesses, like the local auto mechanic, it makes sense to visit the local Chamber of Commerce, but for those companies that target doctors as clients, a pass to the golf course might be a better idea.

The trick is to know where your potential clients are and show up there. Go to the places often enough that relationships can be built. A good guideline is to pick two organizations and commit to them. One is a weekly organization, and the other is once a month. Keep in mind, this suggestion is for businesses with a low turnaround. If your business is structured with high numbers and high turnaround like an auto mechanic, the networking may need to increase.

Remember that the idea, when you show up, is not how many people you can sell to, but how many people you can build a solid relationship with.

Determining Your Networking Strategy—What's the Best Choice for Your Time?

One of the best ways to grow your business is by networking. The reason being you can leverage your connections and be able to more easily reach your target market faster and with more credibility. But how do you know which areas are the best places to network, and how to best use your limited time and money?

To unravel this mystery, determine who your ideal client is. Review your current client list, applying the Pareto principle or better known as the 80/20 rule. The rule basically means 80 percent of your results comes from 20 percent of your effort. The trick is to figure out the 20 percent of actions that will give you more results.

Identify the 20 percent of your clients that are giving you 80 percent of your income. What do the clients have in common? Demographics? Industry? Lifestyle?

After you identify the basics, drill down on where to find prospects who have similar attributes.

I worked with an insurance agent through this process. He developed a spreadsheet and was able to determine his top 20 percent of clients, and to his surprise, they weren't who he was focusing on in his outreach.

He quickly made a shift and was able to increase his income by a third in the next 30 days. Most of that was a result of refocusing his efforts onto a different demographic and onto his marketing strategies. His networking groups didn't change, but how he positioned himself and who he talked to did.

Another client used this system. Her niche was stay-at-home moms. After we made an in-depth study of her business and where she wanted it to go, it became very clear that the best place for her to hang out was not her local business group, but McDonalds, specifically at the playground.

She made the shift and soon found she was able to sign up a lot of mothers every time she visited McDonalds. During her time socializing with the mothers, it was natural for her to introduce her product, which solved the problems for those types of moms.

After you figure out where your potential clients go and have a consistent practice of hanging out there, too, the next place to look at in your networking is your associations. I recommend that people attend an association in their industry. It is important to stay on top of the industry trends, to know what others are doing, and to have colleagues who are friends that you can turn to when you have too much work or you have work-related questions.

If there is a seminar or workshop that your ideal prospects or peers would attend, it might be beneficial to go if you have the opportunity to meet and mingle with other attendees. The ability is important to determine if the event is being hosted online. If there is no ability to meet or reach out to others, it might not be in your best interest to attend. No matter if the event is online or in person, if you are going is critical to have a plan on how you will prequalify prospects and possible joint venture partners.

It is important to be extremely selective with seminars. They cost a lot of time, money, and energy. But some seminars are business-changing. I have met high-level clients and strategic partners at these events that made a huge difference in my business.

No matter if you are networking at your local business chapter, global virtual chapters, seminars and workshops, or attending associations, it can be a huge time sucker or critical to your business growth. If you are going to use the strategy of networking, be conscious about how you show up and approach these opportunities.

Extreme Value of the Right Mentor

In addition to supercharging your network, finding a great mentor can dramatically grow your business. Many entrepreneurs at first are resistant to this. They are independent and are determined to chart their own course. They have a level of independence required and possess a lot of grit. Grit is a must. But from the entrepreneurs I interviewed, being too independent and not seeking out the right help was a common theme that was keeping them from moving forward and something each one them overcame.

Consider Rob Ruder's experience:

"If you build it, they will/won't come (maybe)." I started my business with a mission to change the way people related to technology. I thought my passion would infect everyone around me, that they would point me to friends, acquaintances, or businesspeople who would make my dream come true.

Fifteen years into business, I was still struggling. That was when I became a student of business. A long-time mentor introduced me to Seth Godin and that led me to the world of marketing. I studied SEO, systems thinking, online course building, and direct marketing. Each was an adventure on its own, many of them not cheap, but in the end those experiences led me to a new circle of friends, mentors, and peers who have helped me achieve my original financial goals.

I'm a 20-year "overnight" success!

—Rob Ruder, Software and IT Consultant,
MIC Professor of Systems

Notice in Ruder's experience, he thought that his mission was compelling enough that it would naturally drive business to him. He was in the game working hard but struggling for 15 years until he sought out the right mentors. For him, it wasn't one mentor that made a difference, but many who taught different elements and aspects of his industry.

Ruder sought to learn from the people who were at the top. I did the same thing when I was starting out. I reasoned that learning from the people who were at the top of their game would be more beneficial than from others. Since then, I found that learning from a combination of people at the top of their industry and those who are closer to where I am in business is a better formula.

One of the advantages of being in the sphere of people at the top of their industry is it is helpful to witness and experience that level of professionalism, thinking, and execution. By being in that world, it raised my level of expectation and expanded my thinking and knowledge base. The people at the top of my game thought differently and looked at different patterns and metrics than I was aware of.

Despite all the advantages of working with the top industry leaders, there are also advantages to working with people who are one or two steps ahead of you. The experts that are closer to your success level have a fresher memory of your current challenges and what it took for them to overcome those obstacles. It may have been too long for the people at the top of their game to remember what it was like. In addition, the playing field has drastically changed since they were starting out. Someone closer to your level is more accessible and is able to give more customized attention. Sometimes, it is a little tweak or shift in the way you do things that can make all the difference.

Whether you find your mentors who are at the top of their game or you work with someone that is a few steps ahead of you, or you do a combination, the critical part is the mentors you work with provide you with the right education for your stage of business.

Too many times, the mentors are giving advice that won't serve where the person is at. The stage of business that you are at must always be considered before the advice is given. If that stage is not considered, it can blow up in the entrepreneur's face.

For example, there was a small company who was able to land national exposure. The company didn't have the back-end systems in place on their website to handle the increase traffic. Nor did they have the business marketing funnels and next steps set up. The national exposure hurts their business not helped them because they weren't ready.

It takes time to build out solid workable funnels. Throwing something together to handle the increased traffic would not be nearly as effective as taking time to test market and make sure your offerings are viable to your prospects.

Application Corner

Exercise #1: Strategy for Business Conferences

Before attending more seminars, here are some good questions to ask yourself:

- Can I afford it?

No, don't go. If yes, will I be able to generate enough profit from attending to make attendance worth it? If not, is the skills and knowledge I will be learning the thing I need to go to the next level?

- Can I afford the time off and the time away from work?
- How much of what they are going to be teaching do I already sufficiently know?

This you might have to guess at. If you have been attending seminars and workshops regularly and you are finding yourself bored because you already know most the stuff being taught, chances are you are not going to be missing anything if you skip this workshop or seminar.

Exercise #2: Prepping Before Attending

How you show up to networking events and the preparation taken before attending will make a big difference on the results you will achieve.

Step #1: Determine that the networking group has the opportunity of being a high value for you to attend.

- Will your ideal prospects be there or ideal joint venture partners?

- Is the price of the event within your budget?
- Does the event reflect the values of the way you like to do business?

Step #2: Research the active members and create a list of the top three people you would like to connect with. Determine the value you can bring those people and common interests you may have.

Step #3: Determine your top three goals you have for each networking meeting you attend.

For example: Talk with Sarah and see if she would be open to having a coffee to explore how we could support each other.

See if Ted needs another vendor at his upcoming seminar.

Talk with Dawn about her company and look for ways you could refer her service to your clients.

Step #4: Come up with a strategy for positioning yourself and how you will stand out from the crowd.

Network groups are a great way to test your marketing message. When you pitch it, do people respond or do you receive a glazed response? Do people remember what you do or do you have to explain it.

Step #5: If you are attending an in-person event, before and after the networking is the most valuable time. Do not use it as a social hour. Be deliberate about who you talk to and be on constant look out on how you can serve them and help their business grow.

Exercise #3: Finding the Right Mentor

Ask yourself the following for choosing a mentor:

1. Do I resonate with the teacher?
   Do I feel that he or she can really relate to my situation?
   Does she or he have real life experience that they are teaching from, or is their information based on some theory that they learned from school or books?
2. Do I believe that what they are teaching is critical for me to get to where I want to go?

3. Will I become a better person for learning it and is the knowledge transferable to other areas of my life?
4. Is this something that I can commit to and continue with even if things become uncomfortable or challenging? Are the benefits worth the temporary discomfort that taking action requires?
5. Will this course encourage me to put in the solid structures that will assist me in becoming a better person than I am today?

Making the right decision comes down to feeling a yes in each of these areas or feeling deep inside that nervous twitter inside that says go for it.

SECTION 3

Pulling It All Together

CHAPTER 7

Baby-Stepping Around Mistakes and Toward Success

When someone comes from the corporate world, many struggle with the open nature of being an entrepreneur. When you start your own business, you have no outside structure telling you what to do when. Often this is what you wanted but having a lot of open space can be unsettling.

Many business owners begin by taking classes and listening to lectures of what they should do or what great technique is going to solve their problem. Attending these educational courses and lectures can be incredibly helpful but also has the downside of becoming overwhelming.

Feeling overwhelmed is the result of thinking you have to do a ton of things all at once and not knowing where to start. The best way to avoid feeling inundated with information is to achieve clarity. To do that you need to stop impulsively running your business and drill down on what you want to create and who you want to serve.

So far to date, I haven't met a business owner who couldn't use more clarity, including myself. When you take the time to become crystal clear on how you want your company to look, feel, and operate, you will be rewarded with faster results.

Oftentimes, owners have the general sense of what they want to do in their business, but when they drill down even more as to why they are doing it, what outcome they want, and what the results will mean for them and what the results will mean for their clients—the more juiced they become. The clarity gives the ability to make better decisions.

Everything becomes filtered through the specific vision that you have. When you have this guidepost to direct you on where you are headed, it is easier to make decisions which in turn decreases stress.

A lot of beginning entrepreneurs think that everything is important from getting their websites up, sales funnel in place, accounting set up to social media, and so forth. This isn't true. The first important item to pay attention to is: Are you covering your bills? Most people starting out are not. No shame with this. It is the nature of the beast. Until you are out of the red, the most important thing you can do is bring in more money.

That doesn't mean finish your website. That doesn't mean learn a new skill. That doesn't mean figuring out all the various social media channels. That does mean hop on the phone call with prospective clients and keep calling until you have enough work coming in you are covering your bills.

If your bills are paid, then it is time to look at your goals, systems, structures, and long-term aspirations, both for your business and life. But also consider which strategy is the most logical based on your reality. For example, too many entrepreneurs spend many hours launching their own podcast show when they lack the audience following. First things first. Build the audience, have raving fans, and then engage in podcasts to keep contact with your current clientele. Be a guest on other shows for leverage and exposure. Don't do a podcast before you have a solid audience. It will be a waste of time.

How to Figure Out Your Perfect Work/Life Balance

Part of solving the clarity answer is knowing your personal work/life balance. Not that balance is really achievable, but having your work support your lifestyle is. There is a power principle that helps with work/life balance; it's what I call *zone play*. Zone play is doing things that put you into the "zone," your peak performance in your work and your personal life.

Have you ever found it difficult balancing two different areas of your life, such as work and family? Would you be interested in knowing that there is a way to be happier in both areas—and that it doesn't necessarily require more work?

You should have been there when I was coaching a young sales rep with a truckload of ambition, saddled with the concerns a young family can bring. When he showed up for his coaching call, he announced that his child was in the ICU for an extended stay. He worried how he would he manage the increased family responsibilities along with the constant pressure of having to provide for them. He would have significantly less time for business but a dramatic increase in demand for money because of mounting hospital bills.

To add another layer to his pressure, his wife suffered with a chronic health condition that the doctors said needed immediate attention. The last layer of stress was his own health. He was starting to not feel very good. He wasn't taking proper care of himself.

I immediately had him take a deep breath, letting go of as much stress as he could. Then he quickly wrote down what *needed* to be done in one column and what could be taken off his to-do list in the other. He had to be ruthless. He had no time or energy to work on things that "would be nice to do." Every item in the second column went to the calendar as things to do *after* he climbed out of survival mode.

We then explored what his perfect working conditions would be. This meant in the ideal world what would his work life look like.

The questions I put to him were:

If he could work any way he wanted to, what would be his perfect working conditions?

What things would need to be in place for him to be at peak performance?

How much family time did he need to put in so he wasn't riddled with guilt?

What else did he need in place?

Are there certain people, activities, or meetings that naturally motivate him?

These questions sound easy, but amazingly, many people don't know the answers. After I put my young sales rep through the questionnaire, it became clear that proper food, exercise, and hunting were the magic ingredients to relieve enough stress that he could move through the other challenges with a clear head.

We brainstormed how he could accomplish more of these restorative approaches within the confines of his circumstances. He put more restorative activities in, and the result was he more easily slipped into the zone when he was at work. In fact, at the end of the year, he was ecstatic that he'd worked less than ever but had made significantly more money.

How to Get Your Mojo Back and Sustain It

Sometimes, entrepreneurs hit the wall of burnout. How does one keep going amid all the stress?

Step #1: Practice Self-Care on Steroids

The more intense the situation, the more your mind, body, and soul require care. Increase your rest, be stricter about eating those veggies and avoiding those doughnuts, and exercise to pump that stress out of you. Your body needs the rest, the fuel, and the release of built-up frustrations.

If you are dealing with clinical or chronic depression, seek help. Now is not the time to lurk around and not find what you need to cope.

Step #2: Home in on Strategy

After taking care of the crucial basics, it's time to strategize on the most essential activity for your business and your life. (Sometimes personal issues require the primary attention, and that is OK.)

If you know what the most important activities are, do them. Track your efforts and hold yourself accountable. If you are a bit lost on which direction to go, you might need to explore your values until you have clarity.

Step #3: Uncover Your Top Three Values and Implement Them in Your Business

Don't get caught up in what you think you *should* value (family, God, and so on). Let's assume those are already integrated into your life if they are foundational to you. What we are talking about are those values you need in your business to be at your best. Knowing and honoring your top three values in your business is critical for fulfillment. Awareness of these and keeping them prominent will increase work satisfaction, success, and the ability to maintain your mojo with consistent action.

Now that you are clear on your values; make sure you are honoring what you care about in every strategic project you plan. If your strategy isn't in alignment with your top three values, you will hit gridlock. When you match up self-care with strategy and values, you have a higher probability of gaining and maintaining momentum. You will get out of your own way, plug into your mojo, and produce results.

Uniqueness Equals Value

A part of owning your value may be accepting that you don't fit the mold. To honor who you are can be challenging. There are many business experts claiming that their way is the *only* way. You have to follow their dotted-line path. These experts don't leave room for a person to show up with their unique personality, skill set, and approach. Be wary of these messages that bombard the market. Most of the time, these claims are aimed at getting you to buy their program, which may or may not be helpful for your business.

Some basic guidelines and rules will increase your success, but there is also lots of room for your own unique personality and ability to forge your own touch. Too many people become caught up with running their business the way other sources tell them they have to, down to the smallest detail.

For example, many of the entrepreneurs I interviewed were told that they had to spend hours every day on social media. This can certainly work for some businesses, but it also can be huge waste of time for others.

This advice only serves when your business is ready to support that kind of work and you already have a foundation laid where you know how to best reach your audience. That means your business has the metrics and refined knowledge of who your audience is and knows where they hang out online, what their biggest pain point is, the language they use to express that pain, and what will attract their attention. It sometimes takes years for an entrepreneur to understand these metrics.

Online marketing also will only work for those people who are best at writing and communicating through the Internet or have someone on their staff or independent contractor who excels at this type of positioning.

If you lack the strong writing skills or the funds to pay someone else, your time might be better spent on other parts of your business.

Application Corner

Exercise #1: Business Clarity Audit

Look at your business plan.

Is it specific enough?

Do you know what your main goal is for the next 90 days?

Do you know what business model you are following and which things you most need to learn?

Drill down deep on what it is that you want and where you are going.

A good way to gain this clarity is to answer some of the following questions:

1. What do you most want for your business in the next three months?
2. Why do you want it?
3. What will it do for your business?
4. What other changes will it create for you?
5. What is the biggest obstacle getting in your way?
6. What are three or four creative ways to work around the obstacles?

Conclusion

Each entrepreneur interviewed for this book was willing to be vulnerable and to admit some of their greatest mistakes, allowing for patterns to merge and insights to be gleaned. Others were willing to share their struggles and tell their stories. All of them did so in service to help other entrepreneurs avoid the mistakes they made, for that I am deeply grateful.

These entrepreneurs talk freely about their challenges, mistakes, and solutions. Every conversation was underscored with hope. Not one of them gave up when times became hard; they didn't stop searching for the right answer for themselves, their business, and their clients. They kept at it until, at last, they found a better way to serve.

Making the world a better place is what entrepreneurship is all about. It is a noble pursuit.

APPENDIX

Checklist of Action Steps

Believe in Yourself, Your Company, and Others

- Identify your negative thoughts about yourself and look for evidence the opposite is true.
- Determine your fears and make an action plan for the ones you have control over.
- Make your fears work in your favor.
- Take responsibility for what you are responsible for.
- Do short experiments and receive feedback quickly.
- Look for possibilities.
- Track your business growth.
- Focus on your effort rather than perfectionism.

Know Your Value

- Know the value you bring to the marketplace. If you don't know it, interview your clients, close friends, and family to find out what is special about you and what people need that you have to offer.
- Know how you are different than your competitors.
- Charge what you are worth.

Tell the Truth, Be Forth Right, and Define the Terms

- Be honest.
- Have a strategy on how to handle prospects.
- Construct a contract and spell out all the terms and how things will be handled.

- Show up to business meetings on time.
- Do what you say you will do when you say you will do it.

Take Calculated Risks

- Seek help of lawyers, accountants, and seasoned mentors when assessing risk.
- Gamify your business.
- Remain flexible and keep the ability to take risks.
- Use applied curiosity to every area of your business.

Stay on Top of Your Industry

- Stay on top of current trends in your industry and globally.
- Track the current psychological factors your niche is going through.
- Know what the top topics are being discussed in your industry.
- Read a book a week.
- Have membership in the top associations in your industry.
- Subscribe to leading newspapers and magazines.
- Study your competition.

Anticipate the Future, Predict, and Prepare

- Build a solid retirement plan and ensure that your current business model supports it.
- Be the futurists of your business. Predict what is coming and what you need to be prepared for.
- Watch emerging patterns with your clients, prospects, and on the business front.
- Plan for hiccups such as changing rules on social media platforms.
- Think big and ensure it legally.
- Prepare for volatility even if business is going smooth.
- Work on your soft skills for yourself and developing your employees.
- Use resiliency when times get tough.

Know What You Are Getting Into and Set Yourself Up to Succeed

- Prepare for the time and cost that is involved running your own business.
- Put in structure to deal with the unstructured nature of being self-employed.
- Implement events that keep you building your business and connected to others.
- Determine the best practices for you to manage time and be most efficient.
- Prepare for the gap/plateaus in growth.

Get Into the Game and Own Your Expertise

- Stop any shiny object syndrome you are indulging in.
- Fall in love with your problems.
- Put in guardrails around technology to keep you growing your business.
- Stop playing the Alphabet soup game and get into action building your company.
- Make sure that the conferences and websites you are attending serve your current business and you are implementing what you learn.

Become Knowledgeable on Marketing and Sales

- Charge for your services.
- Understand what sales and marketing strategy you are doing.
- Stick to your sales and marketing strategy long enough to give it a fighting chance to work. Refine it.
- Do a volunteer audit and see where your time is going.
- Capitalize on the power of the nimble.
- Customize your service/product to your customer. Make them feel like you know and understand them.
- Follow up. Follow up. Follow up.
- Do a competitor analysis.

Make It About Your Customer and Prospect

- Do a website audit.
- Stand out in a crowded market.
- Send appreciation cards on odd holidays.
- Know and honor your customers' values.

Understand How People Work

- Establish your RonR.
- Come up with a plan to understand various types of personalities and how to best work with each one.
- Uncover your team motives and the best way to motivate each one.
- Be aware of how you are impacting your team.
- Establish meaningful connections with your client during each touch point you have with them.
- Analyze your sphere of influence and update where necessary.

Adapt Hiring Best Practices

- Have strong system to find the right candidate.
- Implement onboarding system that keeps the business function as training occurs.
- Challenge your hiring biases.
- Have a plan to bridge the hiring gap if you aren't ready to hire yet.

Receive Support

- Build a support network, including mentors.
- Allow help in when needed.
- Work on the skill of receiving support.
- Be generous with your customers/clients.

Set Up Expectations Appropriately for Self, Employees, and Customers

- Build a support network, including mentors.
- Hold weekly CEO meetings.

- Re-evaluate your systems and objectives.
- Ask radical questions.
- Track the metrics in your business.
- Set up supportive expectation on yourself.
- Know your client's expectations of you and put in systems to meet and manage them.
- Practice boundaries with clients.

Transform Into a Business-Growing Machine

- Build a support network, including mentors.
- Demand excellence for yourself and your team.
- Track how you make decisions. Avoid leaning toward your bias.
- Be aware of how you perceive risk.
- Access daily what is most important to focus on.

Stay in Momentum

- Claim the "I did it!" attitude.
- Create or join an accountability group.
- Implement the little habit that will change everything.
- Utilize your motivators.
- Implement excellent self-care practices.

Build a Supportive Environment

- Engage in friendly business competitions.
- Join a mastermind group.
- Set up your work environment to perform at your best.
- Use the most motivating mantra daily.

Supercharged Networking and Mentorship

- Determine your networking strategy.
- Implement a strategy for business conferences.
- Prep before any networking or business gathering.
- Find the right mentor for where your business current is at now.

Baby Stepping Around Mistakes and Toward Success

- Do a business clarity audit.
- Figure out your ideal work/life balance.
- Determine your perfect working conditions.
- Discover your top three values.
- Go forth and serve boldly.

About the Author

Lisa J. MacDonald is an author of 31 books, former radio show host, and business coach for creatives and healers for over 25 years. She was nominated for the Pushcart award 2017 and multi-Amazon bestseller. She earned her MFA in Writing at Antioch University and an MA in English at Arizona State. She assists purpose-driven entrepreneurs to build consistent momentum through clarity, action, and establishing leverage flow. www.StepItUpQueen.com and www.AuthoranastasiaAlexander.com.

Index

Note: Page numbers followed by "n" refer to notes

Accenture Strategic Research Report, 93
Aljets, B., 116
Amabile, M., 117n6
approaches to stay on top of your industry
  follow industry's leading thought leaders, 40
  join the top association in your industry, 39
  read annual industry reports, 39–40
  study your competition, 40
  subscribe to leading newspapers and magazines, 40
Arora, R., 36n1
As CEO You're the Futurist of Your Business (Forbes article), 42
Asp, E., 10n10
Atomic Habits (Clear), 118

Babulic, L., 65
baby-stepping around mistakes and toward success, 144–8, 156
Bailey, C., 60n3
Bain, K., 39n4
Beeby, S.M., 24, 25
believe in self, others, and your company
  doubt and other ways to stop, 8–9
  healthier approach, 5
  idea of stoicism, 4
  not capitalizing on the useful nature of fear, 6–7
  overresponsible trigger, 7–8
  positive side of doubt, 10
  rationalize and prove, 5
  rocky mindset, 10–11
Blasigame, J., 42, 42n5
body-doubling, 130

Bonabeau, E., 110n3
Boudrea, J., 61, 61n5
Bower, T., 30n19
Brownlee, A.L., 117n7
Bryant, A., 31, 31n29
Bullough, A., 47, 47n11

Cacciotti, G., 6, 6n2, 10
Carnegie, D., 9
Ceccato, I., 37n2
Chamine, S., 9
checklist
  about customer and prospect, 154
  adapt hiring best practices, 154
  anticipate the future, predict, and prepare, 152
  baby stepping around mistakes and toward success, 156
  believe in yourself, your company, and others, 151
  build a supportive environment, 155
  calculated risks, 152
  expectations for self, employees, and customers, 154–5
  game and own your expertise, 153
  knowledgeable on marketing and sales, 153
  know your value, 151
  receive support, 154
  set yourself up to succeed, 153
  stay on top of your industry, 152
  supercharged networking and mentorship, 155
  tell the truth, be forth right, and define the terms, 151–2
  transform business-growing machine, 155
  understand how people work, 154
Chitroda, H., 29n18

Clear, J., 118, 119n8
Code of Conduct, 101, 102, 104
Coe, T., 16n11
Cole, C.A., 10n10
Collins, J., 6, 6n3
Colvin, G., 55
criticism and mean people, 46
Crowle, S., 16n11
Csikszentmihalyi, M., 54

Dawson, J., 54n14
Day, J., 81n3
Dean, A.A., 81n3
Dean, S.A., 46n9
deceptions, white lies, and stretching
    the truth
  being late and other questionable
    practices, 23–4
  coaching industry, 21–2
  long-term effects of commitments,
    22–3
  problems with trusting, 24–5
Denburg, N.L., 10n10
Deo, A., 109n2
Di Crosta, A., 37n2
Doyle, A., 45n6
Dravigne, A., 129n5
Drucker, P., 53
Dweck, C., 7, 7n4

East, J.I., 46n9
Effective Executive (Drucker), 53
E-Myth Revisited (Gerber), 42
entrepreneurial mistakes
  deceptions, white lies, and
    stretching the truth, 21–5
  expectations for self, employees,
    and customers, 96–104
  gathering too much information
    and striving for an alphabet
    name, 59–64
  hiring errors, 88–91
  lack a grasp on marketing and sales,
    65–74
  make it about you, not them,
    75–80
  not believing in self, others, and
    your company, 4–14

not knowing your values, 15–20
not looking to others for help,
    92–5
not looking to the future, 42–9
not staying on top of their industry,
    35–41
not understanding how people
    work, 81–7
refuses to take risks, 27–33
unprepared for the time, cost, and
    loneliness, 50–6
entrepreneurs
  experience and feedback, 7
  family commitments, 50
  risks, with no guarantees, 8
  self employment, 3
Evans, B.D., 38n3
expectations
  business owner's responsibility, 99
  client boundaries, 100–2
  client expectations, 102
  mindset play, 98–9
  money, 99
  online signature product, 100
  payment process, 100
  self expectations, 96–8

fear, 6, 8, 10, 11, 27, 30, 60, 82, 98,
    125, 130, 151
Finkel, D., 60, 60n2
Fisic, I., 96n10
Friborg, O., 9n9
Frishberg, E., 8n7
Frost, A., 70n8
future aspects
  changing environment, 46–7
  criticism and mean people, 46
  platform to communicate with
    clients and prospects, 43–4
  soft skills are the future, 45–6
  thinking big enough, 44
  volatile business, 44–5

Gallo, A., 111n4
Gardner, M., 16n11
Gerber, M., 42
Gower, A., 16n11
Great by Choice (Collin), 6

Harvard Business Review (magazine), 61, 94, 119
Hayton, J., 6, 6n2, 10
healthier approach, 5
Henwood, S., 109n2
Hickey, J., 76n12
Hill, N., 125
Hinde, G., 88n7
hiring errors
    bridge hiring gap, 89–90
    money to pay your new hires, 90
    streamline the onboarding process, 90–1
Hole, L., 16n11

Johansson, A., 128, 128n3, 130n6
Jones, L., 30
Jones, R., 107, 108

Kapitan, S., 93n8
Kemper, J.A., 93n8
know your values, 15–19
Koestner, B., 10n10
Kramer, S.J., 117n6
Kulbyte, T., 81n1
Kwik, J., 38

lacking on marketing and sales
    appreciation cards on odd holidays, 79
    competing against the big guys, 67–8
    focus on values your customers, 79
    free service giveaways, 66–7
    guidelines, 76
    marketing and sales efforts, 76
    personal power, 68–9
    power of the nimble, 68
    reality of sales force, 72–3
    short-term panic drives customers, 69–72
    standing out in a crowded market, 77–9
Lawrence, J.H., 112, 113, 113n5
Leonard, G., 55, 55n15
Lineberger, R.D., 129n5
Linkner, J., 8, 8n6

MacDonald, R.C., 27, 28
Manzel, K., 10n10
Marchettie, D., 37n2
mastermind groups
    being in a mastermind group, 125–6
    built in test market, 126
    collective thinking, 127
    deadlines, 127–8
    improved work, 127
    not feeling alone and feeling validated, 125
    track successes, 126–7
McDonalds, R.C., 134
McFuire, L., 130n8
McGuire, L., 130
Millard, N., 16n11
Misner, I., 22n15
money to pay your new hires, 90
motivating fear, 6
Motowidlo, S.J., 117n7

owning your value directly affects your prices, 18–19

Panecasio, S., 130n7
payment process, 100
Peck, B., 88, 89
Peppercorn, S., 7, 7n5
personal work/life balance, 144–6
Picasso, P., 116
Porter, M., 27
Porter, M.E., 27n17
Positive Intelligence (Chamine), 9
The Procrastination Equation (Pychyl), 61
Pychyl, T., 61

refuses to take risks
    acting like a CEO, 31
    applied curiosity training, 32
    decision-making guardrails, 28
    gamification, 29
    stopping the success train, 30–1
relationship skills
    expectations for self, employees, and customers, 96–104

hiring errors, 88–91
not looking to others for help,
92–4
understand how people work, 81–7
Renko, M., 47, 47n11
return on investment (ROI), 81, 84
return on relationships (RonR), 81,
84, 154
Reynolds, P.L., 81n3
Rice, S., 61, 61n5
rocky mindset
believe in self, others, and your
company, 4–14
deceptions, white lies, and
stretching the truth, 21–5
know your values, 15–20
refuses to take risks, 27–33
Rubin, T., 81, 81n2
Ruder, R., 135–6

Sampat, S., 72n11
Sander, L., 119, 119n9
secret weapon of responsibility
adaptive neural network, 109
foundation skill to thrive in
business, 111–12
growth mindset *vs.* fixed mindset,
108
higher risk that comes with age,
110–11
microdecision, 109, 110
radical business questions, 112–13
Sellars, J., 4n1
Shallard, P., 107n1
Simovic, D., 57n1
Sines, F., 124n1
Sleek, S., 54n14
The Sociopath Next Door (Stout), 82
Sooalu, G., 109n2
Spry, A., 93n8
Stangel, L., 9n8
stay in momentum
accountability, 117–18
power of small little actions,
118–19
refueling motivation, 119–21
surge capacity, 121

Stobierski, T., 18, 18n13
stoicism, 4
Stout, M., 82, 83n4
stress burnout
home in on strategy, 146
practice self-care on steroids, 146
uncover your top three values and
implement in business,
146–7
supercharged networking and
mentorship
determining your networking
strategy, 133–5
extreme value of the right mentor,
135–7
supportive environments
color perfection, 129
competition and the power of
being stretched, 124–5
hearing a beat help, 129–30
hidden magic of a simple phrase,
130–1
lighting environment, 128–9
mastermind groups, 125–8
room of inspiration, 128
Sutherland, J., 128n2

Talent is Overrated (Colvin), 55
Tartakovsky, M., 98n11
Think and Grow Rich (Hill), 125
Tranel, D., 10n10

understand how people work
awareness of the impact on your
team, 84
burning bridges, 82–3
cultivating your inner circle, 85–6
meaningful interactions with your
clients/customers, 84–5
not understanding peoples work,
83–4
uniqueness equals value, 147–8
unprepared for time, cost, and
loneliness
fighting isolation in the workplace,
52
time and self-improvement, 54–5

time management, 53–4
time schedule freedom, 51–2

Verplanken, B., 9n9
Vredenburg, J., 93n8

Waliczek, T.M., 129n5
Wang, C.E., 9n9
Weltman, B., 72n9

Wichman, A., 8n7
Wittenberg-Cox, A., 94
Workplace Productivity Statistics
        That Will Blow Your Mind
        (McGuire's article), 130

Zajicek, J., 129n5
Zhao, Q., 8n7
zone play, 144

OTHER TITLES IN THE ENTREPRENEURSHIP AND SMALL BUSINESS MANAGEMENT COLLECTION

Scott Shane, Case Western University, Editor

- *The Hybrid Entrepreneur* by Kevin J. Scanlon
- *Stuck Entrepreneurs* by Jay J. Silverberg
- *Teaching Old Dogs New Tricks* by Thomas Waters
- *Building Business Capacity* by Sheryl Hardin
- *The Entrepreneurial Adventure* by Oliver James
- *So, You Bought a Franchise. Now What?* by David Roemer
- *The Startup Masterplan* by Nikhil Agarwal and Krishiv Agarwal
- *Managing Health and Safety in a Small Business* by Jacqueline Jeynes
- *Modern Devil's Advocacy* by Robert Koshinskie
- *Dead Fish Don't Swim Upstream* by Jay J. Silverberg and Bruce E. McLean
- *Founders, Freelancers & Rebels* by Helen Jane Campbell
- *The 8 Superpowers of Successful Entrepreneurs* by Marina Nicholas
- *Navigating the New Normal* by Rodd Mann
- *Time Management for Unicorns* by Giulio D'Agostino
- *Zero to $10 Million* by Shane Brett

Concise and Applied Business Books

The Collection listed above is one of 30 business subject collections that Business Expert Press has grown to make BEP a premiere publisher of print and digital books. Our concise and applied books are for...

- Professionals and Practitioners
- Faculty who adopt our books for courses
- Librarians who know that BEP's Digital Libraries are a unique way to offer students ebooks to download, not restricted with any digital rights management
- Executive Training Course Leaders
- Business Seminar Organizers

Business Expert Press books are for anyone who needs to dig deeper on business ideas, goals, and solutions to everyday problems. Whether one print book, one ebook, or buying a digital library of 110 ebooks, we remain the affordable and smart way to be business smart. For more information, please visit www.businessexpertpress.com, or contact sales@businessexpertpress.com.

www.ingramcontent.com/pod-product-compliance
Lightning Source LLC
Chambersburg PA
CBHW061314220326
41599CB00026B/4870